Dear Comrades
Readers' Letters to Lotta Continua

Dear Comrades
Readers' Letters to Lotta Continua

Translated by Pete Anderson and Hilary Partridge
Edited and annotated by Margaret Kunzle

Pluto Press

This edition first published in 1980 by Pluto Press
Limited, Unit 10 Spencer Court, 7 Chalcot Road,
London NW1 8LH

This translation © Pluto Press 1980
Original edition copyright © Edizioni Coop.
giornalisti Lotta Continua

ISBN 0 86104 306 5

Cover designed by Kate Hepburn
Cover photo: *é il 77*

Photoset by Photobooks (Bristol) Limited,
28 Midland Road, Bristol
Printed in Great Britain by Lowe & Brydone Limited,
Thetford, Norfolk

Introduction

At its 1976 conference in Rimini, the Italian revolutionary organisation Lotta Continua dissolved itself, but the editorial collective which produced its newspaper (also called *Lotta Continua*) decided to keep the paper going. The absence of an organisation did no harm to the paper's circulation – on the contrary it grew, one of the reasons being the daily Letters Page where comrades no longer in political organisations expressed their views and engaged in debate and discussion.

In 1977, 8000 letters were sent for publication to *Lotta Continua*. Just over 1000 were published and of these a selection of 350 came out in a book *Care Compagne, Cari Compagni. Dear Comrades* is a translation of some of these 350 letters – those that do not require too great a knowledge of the Italian political scene and which take up issues being faced by politically active people in this country.

A State of Crisis

Since 1975, many of the organisations of the far left in Europe have been in crisis. There is no short and snappy explanation for this, but one essential factor is the decline of working-class militancy that occurred with the onset of the economic recession in 1975. The large majority of the far left had been introduced to revolutionary politics in a period (since 1968) when it was commonly believed that revolution in Western Europe was on the cards in the *short-term*, a not unreasonable belief especially in Italy where the far left was the largest in Europe – with three organisations having a membership of over 10,000 each and daily newspapers with a circulation of around 30,000 each.

In the general elections in Italy in 1976, the total of votes cast for revolutionary candidates was 800,000. This performance, which would have been taken as a victory in any other European country, was experienced on the Italian far left as a stunning defeat.

Important Victories

In the period between the Hot Autumn of 1969 and the elections of 1976, the far left in Italy won many fundamental victories and were taken very seriously by the ruling class. In fact, seriously enough for some of them to finance fascists who carried out a series of murderous bomb attacks on the general public that then served as a pretext for the government to put into operation its 'strategy of tension', that drastically narrowed the political space within which the far left could operate. Amongst the victories of the far left, was the recognition by management of factory delegates (shop stewards elected by both union and non-union members), important concessions in government housing policies and the successful referenda on divorce and abortion in which the far left together with the Radical Party played a key mobilising role. However, although it could not be seen at the time, these were not victories that marked a revolutionary break with capitalism but victories that brought Italy from being a backward to an 'advanced' capitalist country – what was achieved already existed in other European countries.

These successes could not satisfy the expectations of revolutionary change held by the members of organisations who were constantly being encouraged by their leaders 'to make one more effort and sacrifice'. As long as they thought that revolution was around the corner, most militants were prepared to postpone their desire for personal liberation. But when the prospect for immediate revolutionary change receded, the demands of the personal swept aside the idea of the revolution-as-sacrifice that had been dominant until then.

Personal Liberation and Feminism

In Italy, as elsewhere, it was feminists who first broke with the ideology of sacrifice and brought the demands of the personal into the political arena. The feminists brought with them a view in which state ownership of the means of production was in no way a

vi

guarantee of personal liberation. The history of this century is littered with revolutions that have done nothing positive about the oppression of women. With their insistence that 'the personal is political' the feminists directly challenged the point-of-production orientation of the far left groups and their unshakeable belief in the 'centrality of the factory'. In other countries, far left groups have found a way (if only an unsatisfactory one) of reconciling this difference between their feminist and industrial members, but in Italy such a reconciliation was virtually impossible for two reasons. Firstly, the massive presence of industrial workers in the revolutionary left gave enormous credibility to 'workerism' (the idea that the struggle in industry is qualitatively the most important). And, secondly, because Italy is a Catholic country where male domination and repressed sexuality prevail to a much greater extent than in the Protestant countries of Northern Europe. In revolutionary politics, workerism and male supremacy feed off each other. Since in countries like Italy the number of women in industry is low (only a small minority of Italian women go out to waged work) those who stress industrial conflict automatically downgrade the contribution women make to the class struggle.

The Effect on Lotta Continua

The confrontation between feminists and workerists shook all the groups of the Italian revolutionary left but it totally destroyed Lotta Continua. The confrontation was worse in Lotta Continua because, more than most, it 'put the class before the party'. It had been the only organisation to respond to the new rapidly growing movements of women, the unemployed, gays, proletarian youth and prisoners. Yet there were important conflicts between these different social movements which became more serious as they developed. Had the leaders of Lotta Continua responded to the feminists, disaster might have been averted. But Lotta's leadership did not understand (or did not want to understand) the nature of the feminists' demands.

A State of Shock

The first letters to Lotta Continua were written only a few months after the Rimini explosion and they reflect the state of shock experienced by all the protagonists. They show that what collided at Rimini were different conceptions of the political. On the one side the leaders and the industrial workers (both under-represented in the letter columns) with their traditional idea of politics as matters of state, incomes policy and what is happening to the Communist Party, on the other side, the feminists and a few 'liberated' men who want to discuss relations between comrades, whether there is a communist way of making love and 'pre-political' questions like why some comrades never talk at meetings.

The Armed Struggle

Whilst this dialogue of the deaf continued all through the period of the letters (March–December 1977), another theme became increasingly important: violence – both the violence of fascism and the violence of armed left-wing organisations like the Red Brigades and the Armed Proletarian Nuclei (NAP). In that period, the debate on violence tended to be abstract and polarised. It was a case of 'are you for the Red Brigades or for the state?', which suited the armed organisations who were able to 'guilt-trip' the majority of comrades into supporting them. But by the time Moro was kidnapped and executed (spring 1978) it had become clear to more and more people on the left that such a polarisation could only fit the logic of the ruling class and had to be transcended. 'Neither the state nor the Red Brigades', the position put forward by Lotta Continua at the time of the kidnapping, very quickly got a lot of support.

It is becoming more and more evident that the escalation of violence between the repressive forces of the state and the armed parties is rapidly eliminating the very *possibility* of revolutionary politics which need to be able to express themselves in the open. Right now in Italy any public expression of left-wing views is a risky and dangerous thing. Many comrades have been killed on demonstrations, and last year fascists beat up and shot the Housewives' Collective who were broadcasting their regular programme on the left-wing free radio station in Rome.

In these conditions, it is understandable that people on the left think very carefully before committing themselves to open forms of political activity – especially since at the same time they have more and more doubts about the forms of political activity and organisation they have used for the last ten years. By now, the debate on violence is about different issues than those expressed in this book. There is general agreement that violence will be necessary to bring about revolutionary change but there is sharp disagreement over what form of violence and what its relationship should be to existing social movements and mass struggles. On the left, comrades (especially feminists) are more and more ready to criticise the elitist concept of violence that informs the practice of groups like the Red Brigades. They want to know by what right the Red Brigades decide which acts of violence the masses want, by what right do they talk in the name of the masses.

A More General Critique

This critique of elitist concepts of violence is part of a more general critique of elitist forms of political organisation that is becoming widespread in Italy. Revolutionaries are going through a period of reflection in which they are having to return to the discussion of fundamental questions about the nature of politics – for the answer you give will determine the form of political organisation you think necessary.

The letters in *Dear Comrades* are important because they show the beginning of this process of questioning, a process that is taking place amongst revolutionaries in all 'advanced' capitalist countries as we realise that not only have some of our previous answers been wrong but so have some of our questions.

Pete Anderson

This letter refers to Francesco Lorusso, killed by the police in Bologna on 11 March 1977 and Pietro Bruno, another Lotta Continua activist, killed in a demonstration in Rome on 22 November 1975.

After failure in the June 1976 elections and the collapse of the China myth had left the new left in Italy in disarray – so much so that in November at the Rimini Congress Lotta Continua disbanded – an unorganised force called simply 'the movement' appeared, with strongholds in the universities of Bologna and Rome.

This movement, of varied composition but roughly expressing the demands of 'non-guaranteed' youth – unemployed, under-employed, temporary workers, students – in February 1977 booed the Communist trade-union leader Luciano Lama out of Rome University. The Italian Communist Party (PCI) stigmatised the movement as petty-bourgeois and fascist.

On 11 March 1977 in Bologna the carabinieri, acting on the orders of Minister of the Interior Cossiga (known on the left as Kossiga), intervened in a student quarrel at the university, provoking a fight. Francesco Lorusso, a medical student, was shot dead by a police officer. The protest demonstration turned into a street battle – with attacks against shops and offices – which continued the following day. The university zone was placed under military occupation and guarded by tanks. Those arrested were accused of participating in a planned insurrection.

Throughout 1977 Italy was governed by an all-Christian-Democrat cabinet with the tacit support, called 'non-opposition', of the Communist Party. This arrangement is often referred to in these letters as the 'DC-PCI regime'.

A hard police line in Bologna may have been ordered from Rome to challenge the Communist Party's pretentions to government by embarrassing it in its traditional stronghold. Bologna was the show case of local Communist administration in Italy, supposedly the best run and most democratic city in Europe under the PCI mayor Renato Zangheri, an elegant university professor.

Mayor Zangheri initially deplored the death of Lorusso, then the PCI and trade unions decided to support the police against the students. Francesco Lorusso's funeral had to take place in semi-private and the movement was forcibly excluded – by Communist trade-union stewards – from the official demonstration convened 'against violence' in the piazza Maggiore. The damage suffered by shopkeepers and restaurant owners – expropriated when the university refectory was closed – was repaid from city funds.

The following is the text of a speech prepared by Giovanni Lorusso, the brother of the student killed by the police, which he was prevented from delivering at the official demonstration on 15 March.

When the authorities stoop so low

Bologna

Comrades,

It isn't easy for me to talk about what's happened these last few days, but I think it's important. Francesco Lorusso, Lotta Continua activist, anti-fascist, medical student, is dead, killed by the carabinieri and the government's law and order policy.

It's important to state clearly where the moral, political and material responsibility for this murder lies.

'Communism and Liberation' [linked to the ruling Christian Democrat Party] decided to test their strength last Friday at the university. The four or five comrades who went along to the meeting they'd called were beaten up and thrown out. Then these strange christians, together with the Dean, called the police and carabinieri to protect them from the chants of hundreds of students. That's all there was, chants and slogans. The 'defenders of law and order' arrived and attacked the young comrades on a pavement in via Zambona. They charged and fired, and some of these cold-blooded shots found a target – Francesco fell, shot dead.

I ask all those who, in good or bad faith, have been outraged by the anger which the students have now taken onto the streets, to reflect and to choose between shop windows and human life.

2

There is one thing we must realise: too many people die on Italy's streets. For this reason, and rightly, the mass student movement has decided against violence and vandalism. It has chosen to defend the lives of its militants through mass organisation, militancy, struggles, demonstrations and assemblies.

Think of the violence that the police, directed by the Christian Democrats, have used against the city in the last few days. Think of the violence there is in the armoured cars, the tanks, the unprovoked baton charges! Somebody wants to spread fear and terror in Bologna.

Someone – the government, the Christian Democrats, the employers – wants to crush the students' rebellion against this system; a system which produces, amongst other things, 4,000 'accidental' deaths at work every year. The students in the movement, despite the fear we all feel, haven't given in and have no intention of giving in. Amongst all the difficulties, they've gone to talk with workers in the factories, with the people in the working-class areas, holding thousands of meetings every day in a city guarded by the military and the police.

I know that the murder of my brother Francesco, the armoured cars, the police charges aren't only directed against students, but against all democratic citizens and more particularly against the workers' movement as a whole. That's why I'm speaking here, even though the Christian Democrats are represented at this meeting.

Nor can I forget that His Excellency the Prefect, the representative of the government, issued a shameful order forbidding not only the funeral in the city but also a wake in the funeral chamber in the centre of town. They killed Francesco, but that wasn't enough for them: his body could not be honoured by the mass of his comrades and democratic citizens. When the authorities stoop so low, to such moral baseness, there can be only one answer: hard, militant, mass struggle. Only the departure of the police, the resignation of the prefect, the speedy punishment of the guilty can re-establish a climate of civil tolerance – there is no other solution. There are more than one hundred students in prison, but even if there were a thousand the authorities would not succeed in shutting our mouths, in stopping us demonstrating for our rights, or crushing our protest.

One last thing. Probably a lot of people don't agree with certain forms of struggle practised by the student movement, and we're ready to discuss this with anyone. But even those who disagree can't forget one fundamental thing: comrade Francesco Lorusso died for you too, he died defending not only his own freedom, but the freedom of all. Everyone can choose, here in this square or elsewhere, between the reactionary order of the armoured cars and tanks and the democratic order of the popular masses, with all their problems and contradictions. We've already made our choice, we're all with comrade Francesco and with the hundreds and hundreds of comrades killed over the years by police bullets while they were demonstrating in the streets.

We workers are different from you

Bologna

Dear university students,
We workers writing this letter don't represent the whole working class of Bologna for two reasons: first, because we speak for only the undersigned; second, because it's our own initiative and we haven't asked for nor had orders from the unions about it.

We've tried hard to understand you. What we have understood is that – even if you are sensitive to the working class – we workers are different from you. The events of the past, that is, the various acts of the workers' movement, teach us that the struggle can be carried forward by democratic means with excellent results.

The students, or rather the extremists, by reacting with acts of vandalism, destroying shops or stealing hams, are simply giving both the working class and public opinion the chance to say they're 'fascists' and 'killers' and that 'if the police shoot, then fair enough, they're shooting at murderers'.

Why has it never been possible to call the working class fascist? The reasons are clear. We workers too, we've had comrades killed at peaceful meetings; at Reggio Emilia, Modena [police attack 1960], piazza Fontana [fascist bomb 1969]. These comrades were killed though they didn't break shop windows or burn factories.

After these events, the Bolognese working class didn't stand
4

passively by. It reacted with democratic demonstrations, avoiding clashes with the police. Clashes with the police belong to the past – the carabinieri are sons of the people even if they're pawns of power. So we maintained credibility in the eyes of the general public and gave nobody the chance to call us 'fascists'.

We believe it would have been much better if the students, instead of acting like hooligans, had gone onto the streets in peaceful demonstration and talked with the people, particularly the working class and explained their problems, what it is that's wrong. After all, a lot of workers are the fathers of families and it's in their interest to improve the situation of their children. In this way the students would have the workers with them too – united we win – and nobody could have said they are provocateurs and 'if the police kill them, it serves the students right'.

The reason for this letter is to invite you to meet us, so that we can try to understand why you (not all of you, of course) use helmets, iron bars, bicycle chains, molotov cocktails etc. like the fascists do, whereas we don't use them.

Furthermore, we ask you, when you meet the undersigned, not to give us sermons or lessons on the evils of capitalism and how to fight it. In other words, we ask you not to come on as professors.

We want to meet you so that the slogan shouted on student demonstrations can really become true: 'Students and workers, united in struggle.'

A group of workers living in
via Guerrazzi 14
(17 signatures follow)

When a comrade dies

Tiela

Dear comrades,
When a comrade dies, when a comrade you don't know is killed, a comrade who lived hundreds of kilometres away from you, the first reactions are of shock, of thinking what should or could be done: manifestoes, leaflets. Then you begin to think, to try and

5

imagine how Francesco lived, what he did, how he thought, who he was.

And I almost feel as if I knew him.

And I get angry because for the Prime Minister it's all normal and inevitable, because the media start talking about hooligans and guerrillas, because the more or less democratic parties are so busy condemning violence and praising the forces of law and order that they forget and would like us to forget that Francesco is dead, killed by the carabinieri and police.

I don't want to forget Francesco, whom I never knew, just as I don't want to forget the dozens of other comrades we have lost.

I want to write about him and about the others, to remember them.

I didn't know Pietro Bruno.
Would we ever have met?
Perhaps at some demonstration.
Us, looking for money to get back south
Pietro in one of the lines –
would we have smoked together,
talked about the demonstration
And Sicily and Lotta Continua?
Perhaps not!
Now we never can.
I didn't know you, Francesco.
I don't know if we'd ever have met.
At Bologna, a trip.
Or in some other place, a meeting.
Would we have eaten together,
and drunk and joked and talked?
Who knows if your Bari accent
could still be heard under a northern veneer?
Perhaps none of this would ever have happened.
Now it never can.
Now it never can.
Because now I know you.
You, Pietro and you, Francesco,
and Tonino and Claudio,
and others, and many others,

6

I know you in death.
Murdered!
By the State murderers!
Your name, your face,
now they're familiar to me,
and I wish they weren't.

Dario

On 12 March 1977, the day after Francesco Lorusso was killed in Bologna, a national protest demonstration was held in Rome. It was raining hard and the city was deserted, but the military forces lined up against the 100,000 demonstrators were the largest ever seen. Sections of the marchers smashed shop windows and burned cars. There were battles with the police, who made random arrests. After this day of violence, political demonstrations were forbidden in Rome indefinitely, preventing even the traditional May Day parade.

Witnesses in Rome

From comrades who went on the demonstration of 12 March, I've collected some testimonials which I give below:

At about 11 p.m. there was firing inside the station, provoked by plain clothes police chasing comrades who had retreated onto the trains. A comrade from Cosenza can witness this. I'm going to write about what happened after the plain clothes police started firing in front of the station. Most of the comrades took shelter in a hotel not far away, including a group from Bergamo. Their coach was parked near a police van and the driver refused to go and pick them up. The Cosenza coach went to get them a few at a time. At a certain point they were stopped by the police. An officer got onto the coach, waving a loaded machine gun . . . He shouted it would fire 650 bullets a minute and pulled the safety trigger back. He shouted that the comrades were worse than fascists, in fact they were fascists, provocateurs, vagabonds, within a year they'd all be sent to labour camps, though they were defended by the stinking rich like Lorusso [the son of a retired carabiniere general]. He shouted to the comrades to let him look them in the face, he made no searches and he got off the coach.

As information this has lost much of its meaning by now, given the far more serious things which have happened all over Italy. However I think that from a political point of view it can be useful for understanding the sort of propaganda the police are fed with, and their reactions. That's all.

Best wishes,

Raffaele Principe

'Guests' of a Roman family

Trento

During the night of Saturday 12 March, in the inferno let loose by the police who had deliberately been given a free hand, four of us – Romeo, Marina, Oliviero and Rosi – together with others, were given shelter by a Roman family. Dozens more comrades were upstairs with another family. They gave us everything: blankets, hot water bottles, coffee, cognac, sleeping bags, macaroni for everyone, blue jeans, socks, etc. They let us listen to Radio Citta Futura [the free radio station] and watch television and use the telephone.

This was not a particularly politically conscious family, they seemed closer to the Communist Party than anything else. Evidently, though, they'd decided whose side they were on – that is, with the 100,000 in the streets, despite their criticism of the wrecking activity of some 'marginal elements'. I believe, though I could be wrong, that there were a great many families in Rome actively in favour of the movement. We saw plastic bags thrown down from the houses, for comrades to shelter from the rain. And pieces of lemon for the tear gas. It would be interesting to find out how widespread such solidarity and active support was in the Roman population on 12 March.

Romeo and Marina

8

After the Chilean coup in 1973, the Italian Communist Party formally announced its new policy of seeking an 'historical compromise', that is, a form of collaboration with the Christian Democrats who had governed Italy since 1946. Following this conciliatory line, the PCI in parliament supported government measures like public financing for political parties, a compromise abortion bill which did not respect a 'woman's right to choose', and more extended powers to the police.

The 'Autonomists' and 'Metropolitan Indians', referred to by the writer represented the two contrasting wings of the movement, one 'violent' and the other 'creative'. The Metropolitan Indians, the most spontaneous and least 'politically conscious' component of the movement, took up the French slogan of May 1968: 'All power to the imagination' which had previously found little expression in Italy.

Bologna: Why I am not renewing my membership card

To the Secretary of the Communist Party Federation, Bologna, and, for information, to *Lotta Continua, Il Manifesto* and *Il Quotidiano dei Lavoratori*

Dear comrade,
I am writing to inform you of my decision to resign, as I believe is the custom. By now I should have renewed my membership card. But the party's attitude to the Bologna events, following other decisions (state financing for political parties, abortion, school reform, public order etc.) has made me decide against it.

When I think about what happened after the death of comrade Lorusso, I feel violently angry at the stupidity shown by the party. On Saturday morning I was at the demonstration in piazza Maggiore, and seeing the PCI stewards I understood that our strategy of opposition to the student movement was absurd, dictated by a policy of conciliation towards the Christian Democrats which would inevitably lead us to accept repression. One can't hide behind the trite analysis that calls the students 'fascists', paid provocateurs, because this movement – the Autonomists, the Metropolitan Indians – expresses real anger, real social disintegration and a lucid awareness of the function of control over the working class assigned by capitalism to the Communist Party. *We*

9

are supposed to represent 'social-democratic' order, good for the shopkeepers and bosses big and small, while *they* represent subversion, extremism, the wicked wolf in fairy tales.

On Sunday, with the arrival of the tanks, the unjustified police attacks, the indiscriminate arrests, the statements of [the Communist mayor] Zangheri, I had no further doubts: the Christian Democrats have landed us of the PCI with the political responsibility for the deliberate repression now being carried out by the servants of Cossiga [the Minister of the Interior].

Dear comrades, the working class knows that 'special laws' are used only to screw it. History has taught us that.

Certainly you could ask me why I rejoined the party in 1972, just when the policy of 'historical compromise' burst onto the scene. But I think it's hardly necessary to explain that what decided so many of us to re-enter was the conviction that through discussion and political work we could help push the party 'to the left', re-establishing a real link with the needs expressed by the working class through the – often contradictory – positions of comrades outside the party.

However, in the last few years I've observed that the party is in fact moving further and further away from a class position. The lack of discussion, the exclusion of dissenters and the consequent impossibility of changing the party line, if not on a national at least on a local level by our daily practice, have rendered my choice to stay in the party futile. I'm only sorry that today, when I have taken such an important decision, some people see me as one of the 'new police' because up to now I've been a member of this party which treats comrades as 'outsiders' in the same way that the ruling class segregates 'madmen' and 'criminals' from the rest of society.

I wish I could make a clearer analysis in a more suitable, more political style, but I can't. I just feel angry and sad.

Communist greetings, hoping that we'll meet again in the struggle for communism.

Maria Pia Garibaldo, trade union delegate

Autonomia Operaia (Workers' Autonomy) represented the 'violent',
10

organised wing of the movement, initially predominant, then in-creasingly criticised by the other components in the course of 1977. Many of the following letters complain about Autonomia's behaviour during street demonstrations.

The actions of Autonomia were based on an analysis of contemporary capitalism as a form of power diffused throughout society, rather than concentrated in the large industrial complexes. The revolutionary protagonist of the struggle against capital is no longer the organised industrial worker, but a new figure, the so-called 'social worker', defined by his or her general situation of oppression. The category also covers 'non-guaranteed' workers, and women. The contradiction between the 'social worker' and capital-ism is direct and cannot be mediated; all existing political parties and the trade unions function only to suppress the contradiction. Any clash directly expressing social needs (including actions like absen-teeism, factory sabotage, mass looting, known as 'proletarian expropriation', etc.) challenges state power and is ipso facto *political. During 1979, with the arrest of Toni Negri and other well-known theoreticians and leaders of Autonomia, the Italian magistra-ture tried to establish a false link between Autonomia and the armed terrorism of the Red Brigades (BR).*

Although Autonomia refused to participate in existing institu-tions, it was not against organisation as such and tended to constitute itself as a classical Leninist party, in contrast to Lotta Continua, by 1977 committed to the idea of a movement. An important clarification between the various tendencies in the movement took place in Bologna the following September (see page 110).

Don't fuck up class unity!

Rome

I'm an under-employed comrade close to Lotta Continua, and I want to comment on the demonstration of 12 March [in Rome]. I got the feeling that a nasty disease is spreading inside the movement: cretinism, a disease once confined to the so-called 'Autonomia', but now catching on. I'm referring to the various acts of damnfoolery during the demonstration, 'justified' by those concerned because 'we're repressed', 'angry', 'there's a feeling of

11

rage'. Sure, I'm repressed too (on the sexual-emotional level and all the others). I'm angry too, because I can't find a job, and for lots of other reasons, and because yet another comrade has been murdered by the state killers. Who the hell isn't angry and repressed? But if all the 100,000 comrades on the demonstration on Saturday had vented their anger like that, all the shop windows and cars of central Rome wouldn't have been enough, we'd have had to go to the most distant suburbs.

The progress of revolution isn't a game, nor is it psychological therapy in which everyone stupidly vents their personal fury in the streets. Otherwise we're guilty of a deep contradiction, talking about bringing consciousness to the mass of workers and then doing shit like this which they can't identify with and criticise. Let's remember that when the masses become radically conscious they'll pick up the gun too. In this phase, if we play it right, there can be a growth and consolidation of the class movement.

The contradictions within the Communist Party rank and file and the revisionist groups are exploding. It's our job, as real communists who believe in working-class unity, to work towards the construction of a homogeneous movement which can find unity of action in class-based opposition to the DC-PCI government.

If fewer stupidities had been committed over the last couple of years – and Autonomia holds a record here – I think that right now the movement would be further ahead. Comrades, I want to change this lousy society, but not in 60, 70, 80 years time, because I won't be here then. So if we really believe in communism, let's stop this shit, let's try to use our anger differently.

Communist greetings,

A comrade

Settling accounts all round

Cameri (Novara)

Thursday the 24th was an important day for us Fiat workers, for the first time we went through the offices in a mobile picket. But I want to tell the story properly.

Already on Tuesday, the first shift, considered the strongest,
12

had had an internal demo, representing the anger accumulated over the past few months; anger towards the government, towards Fiat which has appointed as chief personnel officer a fascist like Davico, who's made life impossible inside the factory; anger about our situation – we still don't know what is planned for our plant. On Thursday we decided on a different form of struggle, the guerrilla strike.

At 7 a.m. the whistles and a comrade's megaphone announced the strike. The workers' response was immediate and total, and despite the rain we went straight to the gates which we blocked until 10 o'clock. There wasn't anyone left on the shop floor!

The foreman, Bagnati, tried to get in, when he arrived as usual at 7.10, but he had to wait until 10, together with the office workers. The manager, Davico, who'd been tipped off by the factory guards, didn't show up. In the afternoon, at 4, the second shift started. We decided on an internal demo. After having shut down one line we went to the offices and tried to break in, but a mass of factory guards stopped us, so then we went back to assembly shop No. 1, where a lot of workers complained that we hadn't got into the offices. So then we went back into the courtyard in front of the office block, and found a side door. We got past the guards and up to the offices at last! Over a hundred workers invaded the corridors and began to stamp their feet, shouting 'dummies, dummies!' and 'out, out!' drumming their fingers on the windows of the locked offices. After that we went to the gates, formed up into a wedge shape and forced the office workers, who'd decided to leave, to pass through it (the fear of staying inside until 11 was too much for them). More rhythmic chants, slogans like 'it's time for a shock in the office block' etc.

The demo in the offices was seen as a great victory, a real leap forward in our struggle. But even more important, we've shown a road which all workers will want to follow now: *to go into the office blocks.* Today we gained confidence in our own strength, with this strength we can settle accounts all round, with the government, with Agnelli, our boss, in the negotiations, with anyone who wants to dismantle the plant at Cameri – and why not? – with anyone who lays a hand on index-linked wages.

A Fiat worker

13

Verona is in the 'white' (Christian Democrat) region of Veneto, a centre of neo-fascist terrorist activity in the late 1960s and early 1970s. The 'yellow and blue brigades' mentioned in the letter refer to the colours of the Verona football team.

The organised fan

Verona

Dear comrades,
I'm a comrade who goes to the football ground a lot and feels the debate about sport for the people and the organised fan in a very personal way.

I read the article about the bomb at the Verona stadium which states that it could not have been thrown by local fascists, and I think you're right, or at least not far wrong.

In fact, for the last few years there has been a massive presence of fascist thugs at the ground and unfortunately they've organised around them a small group of fans from the suburbs who vent their anger with shouts of 'Eia-Eia' and fascist salutes.

This is partly the comrades' fault, as they've never understood this phenomenon and have a very superficial view of the football question in general.

Going back to the problem of the fascists, several times they've threatened me and other comrades who've been brave enough to go into their end, where – coincidence! – the bomb probably came from.

At times the stadium has been a meeting place for some well known thugs, including one of the biggest heroin pushers in town. The last time I got involved with them was during the match against Bologna, when some Bolognese comrades were attacked and I just managed to avoid an armed assault.

These fascists proclaim their politics by waving national flags, wearing black scarves and kerchiefs, shouting slogans like 'sex, violence, yellow-blue brigades' and making fascist salutes; all this with the complicity, under a pretence of indifference, shown by the local rag and the president of the club.

To conclude, I'd like to invite comrades from other cities to open a debate on the football phenomenon and particularly on
14

who's behind certain fan clubs like the yellow-blue brigades of Verona.

Radice

I can't believe it, Francesco

Bologna

I can't believe, Francesco,
That you're dead.
I can't believe your eyes
will not see again,
your hands will never hold more
red flags.
And I believe I'll hear
your calm voice again:
form up comrades . . .
I can't believe
your heart is cold,
that your anger
is buried.
I thought I saw you
at your funeral
in the crowd, crying
quietly and hugging
the sad comrades.
But perhaps it was another funeral
one of many
forced on us by this regime.
Do you remember the morning
we saw a black cat die
before our eyes?
We felt strange,
pessimistic. And you said:
how ugly death is!
The cat was in agony,
it was horrible to watch.
I can't believe it, now.

15

I don't believe
that you're dead, too,
young, strong and healthy
always in the front line
always with the comrades.
Why weren't you there yesterday
at the dead comrade's funeral?
I can't believe it, Francesco.

Carla

The 12 March arrests

Rome

Dear comrades,
I'm writing again to ask: how come a paper like ours, a paper of the
'revolutionary left', hasn't written one line, one correct comment,
on the comrades arrested on 12 March, who haven't been
mentioned since the court case? Does it seem right to you, for
example, that not a word has been said about comrade Michele
Molinari whose plaster cast was broken, who was denied hospital
treatment before the trial, who after the sentencing and a brief stay
in hospital was sent back to the infirmary at Regina Coeli prison,
and who, as he is still in military service, will almost certainly end
up at Fort Boccea detention centre? Do we want to abandon these
comrades, who have done nothing wrong, who were just unluckier
than us, and are only guilty of getting arrested in our place?
    With a clenched fist.

Maria Grazia

*On 21 April 1977 the police cleared the university in Rome. Clashes
in the streets followed, during which a policeman by the name of
Settimio Passamonti was shot. During 1977 firearms appeared in the
hands of demonstrators, and also of police agents dressed like
demonstrators. The existence of these 'special squads', officially
denied, was proved by photographs of agents kneeling to shoot.*
    The PCI, condemning the movement, repeated that the police

16

were 'sons of the proletariat', an expression coined by Pier Paolo Pasolini in 1968 against the first student demonstrators. Italian state employees, including members of the various police forces, are in fact recruited largely from the poverty-stricken south.

So many 'why's'

Turin

Dear comrades,

I've been a Lotta Continua activist for a long time. Now I'm in crisis.

On the front page of today's paper I read 'Policeman sent to fire on students is killed in Rome', and a series of squalid, very general articles on what happened the day before in Rome.

A policeman is dead, another son of the southern proletariat, victim of the Kristian-Democrat-Mafia regime. A proletarian policeman who also happened to support police unionisation; one of the people with whom, a little while ago, we were going to start a dialogue. The paper said nothing about this. Why? Of course he was killed by the DC who sent him into the clash with students, but also by 'comrades' who have mistaken the class struggle for a shooting range, a moment of confusion and change in the movement for a pre-insurrectionary period! Comrades who use violence as a habit, even towards other comrades.

The women's movement and the unemployed movement, whose validity and combativity are unquestioned, have never used P38 guns and so-called 'autonomist' methods. Why not? Why does *Lotta Continua* as a paper – since Lotta Continua as a party doesn't exist any more, especially in Turin – defend these people? When the majority of students had decided on a non-violent reaction to police aggression, why were a minority allowed to overturn this decision. Why did the same thing happen on 12 March in Rome? When the major revolutionary organisations existed in a meaningful way this sort of thing didn't happen. Why?

For every comrade, violence is a contradiction. We use violence only to eliminate it, not to replace one form of violence with another.

A while ago, on the issue of militant anti-fascism we used to

17

say 'Only when the objective is really recognised by the proletarian masses, and followed by them, can we talk about militant anti-fascism.' (For example, the fire-bombing and assault on the fascist headquarters by two to three thousand comrades in Turin two years ago.)

Are the actions of the so-called 'Autonomia' part of the class struggle and militant anti-fascism?

Once again, for fear of losing control (in this case, of the student movement), we're taking up wrong positions, positions that aren't ours, that weren't expressed by the Rimini Conference nor by the students' movement.

Revolutionary greetings,

A comrade in crisis

Around 1972 censorship of pornography was relaxed in Italy. The result was a notable escalation in the quantity and hardness of the material produced and publicly displayed by newsagents.

Selling pornography

Milan

Dear women comrades,
I am a woman who works in a Milan newsagent's and I am fed up, really fed up with part of my job – dealing with the mountains of pornography and pseudo-pornography that come into the kiosks every day. This morning 23 new magazines arrived and every morning it's much the same. I have to sort out a heap of publications that offend women, upset me and almost make me feel sick. What can I do about it?

I can't refuse to sell them since I am a retailer and have to sell whatever the wholesaler delivers to me. I can refuse to display them, keep them off the counter, but this isn't enough. I still feel that I'm selling other women and living a double life, that of the feminist and that of the newsagent earning a living. It's particularly difficult on days like today when the printers are on strike and there are no newspapers, but these damn magazines are still

18

around, showing *Lola with the Magic Arse* or *Clara of the Tight Cunt* or *The Bestial Loves of a Thirteen-year-old.*

I am against censorship, but I can't stand selling this stuff any longer. And it isn't only old men or anonymous types that buy them, but comrades as well. Sometimes I hear someone asking for '*Lotta Continua* and *Hours of Lust* please, miss.' To say that I'd like to ram the papers up their arse is an understatement.

I would like the paper to start a debate on pornography, including the 'new pornography' of sadism and violence. I would like people to make these publications go bust by refusing to buy them. I would like magazines that deal with love, happiness, eroticism, – magazines that give joy.

One other point, I am often taken for 'a woman of easy virtue' because I sell these publications. As I was once told, 'Only a whore sells these whorish mags.' So more than once I have had to get myself out of a fix. Not to mention the man who masturbated behind the kiosk, excited by the sight of 'my' magazines. I leave you to draw your own conclusions about a problem that may well force me to change my job.

Patrizia

Delegation, power and women

Together we've read and discussed the article 'Delegation and power amongst women' in *Lotta Continua* (23 April). We think this article is very important because we hope it will start a debate in the movement on these questions. However, we think it's a mystification that the debate should have been opened by those women comrades who have a power base in the movement, because it's really an attempt to lead and control the debate from a single point of view, the point of view of people with power.

These women comrades say that the problem of power in the movement doesn't exist in the sense that our power has no social expression, isn't expressed in any institutionalised way. While we think it's true that a female power, with its own history and culture, doesn't exist, this doesn't mean that we women are immune from using power borrowed from those who have always used it against us. Some of us have borrowed this power and use it

19

in the form of the 'power of words'. Women comrades who claim the power of theorisation are, in fact, only using the 'power of words' to cover up and deny the needs, the claims, the contradictions and the diversity of the movement. For us the 'power of words' means the power of elaboration of thought and language, theorisation divorced from real experience and from dialogue with other comrades. It's a way of presenting oneself as a rational synthesis which takes the spontaneity out of our meetings and prevents us from understanding each other and expressing ourselves freely.

Let's take an example. The 8 March proposal on work made by some well known collectives was an abuse of power. We don't like it that a small group of women comrades should sit around a table discussing the problem of work and then present the movement with the 'theoretical key', thereby contradicting one of the most revolutionary ideas and practices of the feminist movement – starting from one's own personal experience. Moreover, the 'power of words' masks the real political divisions within the feminist movement. In the case in question, this power was used to present the problem of work in a falsely neutral way, in order to get us to take part in the demonstration with the UDI [the Communist and Socialist Parties' women's organisation]. This was against the desire of the majority of sisters who didn't want to separate the expression of their own needs from the struggle at the university in that period. Now, when the police and state have unleashed a violent repression against people who express anti-institutional demands in the streets, we'd have liked to dance through the whole city to take it back for ourselves. Our dances up to now have always been considered picturesque . . .

Annamaria, Ida, Laura B., Laura D. M.,
Mariella, Mirella, Rosa

Lotta Continua was born as an extra-parliamentary organisation in 1968 in Turin, which remained its stronghold. In the following years it had considerable influence in the factories there, particularly Fiat-Mirafiori. The dissolution of Lotta Continua was particularly disorienting for activists in Turin.

20

I'm completely confused

Dear comrades,

I'm a 30-year-old Turin worker and I've been an LC sympathiser from the beginning, since the spring of 1968. In these ten years I've asked nothing from the party and I've always tried to contribute from the outside in some small way – the paper has been my only connection with LC. When I say contribute, I mean collecting money for the paper, collecting for the Chilean comrades in MIR, paper selling, helping with campaigns for persecuted comrades (yesterday Dario Fo) and drumming up support for elections. It was all worthwhile because on demonstrations you'd see more and more people, really committed people, behind the LC banners.

Now I'm completely confused – in Turin LC practically doesn't exist any more. I interpreted the Rimini Conference (I read the book on it eagerly) as a new example of something that's always been typical of us: the courage to question every single assumption in order to go forward on a better basis. But if questioning past assumptions means destroying everything, then I don't understand and I don't agree. Why isn't the situation of LC in Turin and throughout the country being discussed in the paper? Once it was unusual to see people walking around holding our paper. Now I see them every day, young and not so young. This is really nice and its very encouraging to see sales of the paper are increasing (in my area *LC* is always sold out), but it's not enough if it's going to turn into just another newspaper reporting the various struggles in the country while the organisation disappears. Comrades, if my impression is wrong, correct me and I'll be the happiest man in the world.

Ciao,

A sympathiser of ten years' standing

There are no monsters

We want to describe briefly the violence exercised at every level against a woman comrade by a so-called activist of LC; a six-year marriage characterised by frequent episodes of calculated violence, from beating to moral and emotional blackmail and economic exploitation.

This sister has been gradually expropriated of her being as a woman, of her own needs and her own time, forced to dedicate herself completely to the requirements of her comrade/boss. Despite this, our sister T. has managed to break out of her enforced isolation, she's rediscovered a sense of her own life and her own space through solidarity with other women, which has given her the strength to rebel.

Her comrade soon reacted, 'I use your cunt, you use my car.' He tried to stop her relating to other women by using underhand logic, 'I'm not talking about other feminists – for the moment – I'm talking about you, you don't understand a fucking thing.'

At this point the 'comrade' felt the situation was getting out of his control and threw T. out of the house, 'If you want to live in my house give me good sex, otherwise get out.' He claimed that this represented a real choice and that *he* was the victim of *her* violence (?!).

This character refused to consider legal separation, not wanting to break up a convenient set-up which gave him all the legal rights.

Despite our condemnation, other male comrades have taken a purely formal position, refusing to give in on the substance of the question. So the matter has ended there, but we maintain that with their irony and basic indifference these comrades accept and perpetuate the same violence.

Once again we reject the idea of 'monsters', of exceptional cases. That's only a convenient excuse for those who prefer not to examine their own lives, continuing a male conspiracy of silence.

A feminist group at Imola

The Lord of the Rings

Turin

Dear comrades,
I read in today's *Lotta Continua* about how hard it was to make the

22

strike effective in the big plants, particularly at Marghera, but also in many other places. Where I work – Fiat Lingotto – support was very low, particularly on the first shift.

I'm writing because, as usual, the articles went on about the role of the so-called 'vanguard', who should be 'shouldering their responsibilities'. Well, comrades, I think the time has come to say a few things.

First of all, what 'vanguard'? Where are they? I have a vague idea of the size (very small) of the revolutionary left in the other big factories and Lingotto, where there are at least 10,000 workers, is no exception. There are at the most ten comrades here who identify (some more and some less) with the far left, and we are divided amongst ourselves. In the totally bureaucratised factory council there are three and a half of us (that is, one of us is there, but it's as if he wasn't, considering that he never opens his mouth) who provide a revolutionary opposition to the policy of the union bureaucrats responsible for this impasse.

Well, comrades, given this situation, what responsibilities do you want us to shoulder? The truth is that there are very few revolutionaries in the factories; lots have tried to work there, but after a few months they go back to whatever they were doing before.

The crux of the problem is this: either the revolutionary left finds some way of increasing the number of its militants on the shop floor, or asking a non-existent vanguard to 'shoulder its responsibilities' and criticising them because 'they don't take the initiative' becomes senseless, and frustrating for those few comrades who still manage to stand the horrors of factory work, the inhuman shifts etc. Because the 'vanguard' are comrades like the rest, who feel the weight of our contradictions, who don't want to be made to feel guilty. We're tired (at least I am) of being the 'vanguard' which has to 'shoulder its responsibilities', in the same way the Metropolitan Indians are tired of 'having' to be ironic and witty, and the feminists are tired of 'having' to think about liberation, and the gays are tired of 'having' to worry about sexuality, and even the freaks who 'have' to be into hypodermics and joints. We've got to stop this division of roles. I want to be a whole militant fighting for the liberation of the total human being.

23

I want to be vanguard, Indian, gay, freak, and I want to roll joints (I already do).

Regards from a total perspective,

Gandalf the Grey

PS My official name is Saro Gabrotti, but having chosen to be Indian as well I've taken the name of the chief wizard in Tolkien's trilogy, *Lord of the Rings.*

In Italy, compulsory military service is considered a guarantee against the anti-democratic risk constituted by an all-professional army. Recruits serve for 12 months, receiving only nominal payment (500 lire a day, about 35p) so they have to rely on money sent from home.

Lotta Continua, when it existed as a party, was active in the barracks through a movement called 'Proletarians in Uniform'. At demonstrations in the early 1970s there were often a few groups of uniformed soldiers, marching with handkerchiefs over their faces to avoid recognition. In the same period the small Radical Party campaigned for the recognition of the right to conscientious objection, and won a form of alternate 'civil' service.

Discipline 'by George'!

Pontebba (Tuscany)

The new authoritarian turn gradually imposed on our country is beginning to be felt in the barracks too. Various special corps are already being used for internal order. The spread of this tendency means an attempt to achieve a new level of efficiency and discipline in other army corps, which previously could hardly be trusted for this sort of action.

In our barracks and the other units of the 'Julia' Brigade, manoeuvres and alerts have become more frequent. For the first time, a fully-armed battery stays out for three days every week; the armed picket is out in the town at night; half the soldiers stay in the barracks during holidays, ready to intervene in case of an emergency; and the alerts are getting more and more frequent.

24

Naturally, to make us stand these increasingly awful conditions, there's been a toughening of discipline, now at an incredible level, and leave passes are used as a form of blackmail.

The consequences of this tightening up have become dramatically clear. In our barracks, which has a personnel of 300, three attempted suicides have been reported in the last two months. The last happened on Sunday, 24 April, when a fellow conscript decided to finish with this shitty life by slashing his wrists with an army knife in a railway station toilet. He had 26 deep cuts and was saved by pure chance.

Naturally the authorities have tried to keep all this quiet, and we don't know whether the letters we have sent to the local papers will be published.

Another sad, if less tragic, reaction to the situation is the increase of drunkenness among soldiers trying to escape the reality of their hard life – this is presented in a mystified way as part of the tradition of the Alpine troops.

Comrades! This is the brutal daily reality. This is the real face of the mountain troops of the 'Julia'! Not the picturesque, distorted version agreed with the top brass and presented by the popular press.

A group of democratic soldiers

Just like for the big names

Rome

To remember a hero fallen in battle or some famous person who left his imprint is much easier than to remember one of the many who left no imprint, and was never hailed as a political figure. For this reason, a few lines in memory of a 21-year-old comrade who died tragically in a road accident in the morning of 9 March 1977 are of great importance.

His last struggle, perhaps the hardest of all, lasted seven days; the struggle between life and death. During these seven days his comrades waited outside the intensive care unit, day and night, hoping we'd have him back among us more alive than ever before, with all his imagination. In the struggle at the university, in the movement, this unknown comrade was faithful to the communist ideas he'd arrived at on his own . . . at meetings, rallies and demonstrations, the unity of struggle had become concrete for him. This is the promise that we, your comrades and brothers make you: Brunello Innamorati, today your name appears in this paper which was our common banner and today we grasp that flag and wave it high as we did for the big names when we struggled together.

The comrades will never forget you

Image of conspiracy

Bologna

This spring / of half sun / as one / long before dawn / (as soon as the musical box hearts are asleep, the dreams of my / comrades slip through the hedges) / thirty vehicles set out / black black: SDS, carabinieri, Finance Guards / from Bologna to Milan, Rome, Verona, Padua and Venice, / they're looking, speeding in their vehicles with bloodhound breath, / for documentary proof of subversion, plots and criminality . . . / (for other synonyms please see the Bologna University article of 8.5.77.) How funny! / Subversion, criminality, conspiracy sells its image and seeks us out. / Enter a 'conspirator' at my house, carrying the stars, the news, / a package holding the voice of Radio Alice, the Bologna free radio / and other things. Tonight the night of the 'half repression'. / Is Diego sleeping at San Giovanni? / The PCI paints the scenery / perhaps we're leaving for Germany, / a comrade in my bed has gone underground with 'Snoopy'. / We, comrades, are sure / they won't get the chance to catch us. /

Goodbye.

On 12 May 1977 in Rome the Radical Party prepared to celebrate the anniversary of the referendum victory which had introduced divorce into Italy, thanks largely to the efforts of this small organisation dedicated to the non-violent struggle for civil rights. When the demonstration was banned, in line with the general prohibition still in force in Rome, the Radicals announced that they would hold a peaceful sit-in in piazza Navona. The police unexpectedly attacked

26

*the demonstrators and an 18-year-old schoolgirl, Giorgiana Masi,
was killed. The media reported that Giorgiana had been passing by
and got mixed up with the demonstration 'by chance', a version which
tended to shift the blame for a particularly scandalous death away
from the authorities. Films showed that the notorious 'special squads'
had been in action and that agents had deliberately aimed at
Giorgiana, who was isolated. The Radicals and the movement
concluded that the police, afraid of shooting one another, had decided
that they could safely aim at a woman.*

They take away our joy – they take away our lives

I've spent the day going back and forth, with hundreds of other
women, between the general assembly at the Women's House in
via del Governo Vecchio and the place where Giorgiana was
killed. I saw women who were afraid, who kept changing their
minds and attitudes, who denied their own feelings for fear of the
logical consequences. I felt, beyond all the fear, a widespread
desire to find independent forms of struggle and communication
in a besieged city. On the spot where Giorgiana was killed we left
purple and pink flowers, and a sign reading 'The Rome feminist
movement says "No" to a return to normality. The women won't
go home, they'll stay in the streets and struggle.'

We arrived with our flowers in the afternoon, a few at a
time – the people saw us go by but there was no general decision to
stay there. Finally, from 7 p.m. onwards, hundreds of us came
back to sit-in. What can you sing when a sister is killed? We sang to
give ourselves courage, but we couldn't find the right songs and
many of us had lumps in our throats. So we chanted slogans: 'A
city under siege, a girl killed, this is Kossiga's 'law and order', 'Our
violence has never existed – we'll invent it to take back life', 'You'll
pay for this, hang-man Kossiga . . . you take away our joy, you
take away our lives, we'll put an end to this system.' The old
women from the streets around came with tears in their eyes. There
was no feeling of fear, we could have made the sit-in bigger. Traffic
was blocked on the bridge and on the embankment, and all Rome
saw us.

Vida
27

A carpet of flowers

Rome

Yesterday, together with other sisters, I stayed until late evening watching over the place where Giorgiana was killed. As well as pain and sadness for the death of a sister, I felt a tremendous unease about the choice made by part of the feminist movement to stay off the streets and hold a permanent assembly in the Women's House in via del Governo Vecchio instead. It seemed to me that there was real terrorism in the attitude of some women comrades against those in favour of demonstrating our sorrow on the streets.

I don't want to despise fear, or have a superficial, superior attitude towards those who feel it, but I can't agree that any presence in the streets – like yesterday's in piazza Belli – automatically means accepting police provocation, inviting violence and butchery. Can't I even breathe at this point without disobeying government orders? The place where Giorgiana was killed has become a carpet of flowers brought by thousands of people, young and old. I don't want to accept that I'm powerless, I don't want to go on passively putting up with every dirty trick, I don't want to have to go out into the streets with only the male comrades because the women won't come.

D.L.

Giorgiana wasn't there by chance

Yes, this death was absurd, but it has a very precise meaning; it fills us with rage and deep discomfort but doesn't prevent us from lucidly describing both our dead sister and the situation which led to her murder. Giorgiana wasn't in piazza Gioacchino Belli by chance. It would be like saying that we demonstrate, we carry our struggle out onto the streets, not because there's no chance of getting a job, not because we're faced with a future without life and without hope, not because this education certificate is just a worthless bit of paper, not because we live in a climate saturated with violence, but just like that, by chance! Giorgiana wasn't killed

28

by mistake or by chance. These deaths, this climate of terror which induces the desire for 'law and order', for police everywhere – police that shoot – isn't what we students or workers want.These dramatic demonstrations, when everyone calls us criminals and provocateurs, in which Giorgiana has always participated (never turning up by chance) are certainly no good for us.

Everything happens so suddenly, you feel as if you've got nothing to hold on to, nothing to fight back with. But we must fight back, we've got no right to sit and cry, there's no sense in it. This absurd death mustn't increase our confusion, it must make us think and reflect. And not only we who are Giorgiana's class-mates, but everyone, because this death mustn't and doesn't concern us alone. Giorgiana would be the first to say we must carry on the struggle against all anti-democratic decrees – right to the end.

Comrade Giorgiana's men and women classmates

I felt out of place

Rome

I went to the Women's House in via del Governo Vecchio to be with my sisters, to share my anger, my sadness, my desire to claim Giorgiana's death as our own, as the price which women who take the struggle out onto the streets must pay. There were very few of us, no more than three hundred, and the women students weren't there.

The atmosphere was heavy, dominated by fear, impotence, the inability to react fully to events. I was shocked by the general atmosphere of terror and couldn't identify with the speeches calling for a timid response. I wanted to say that for all of us to occupy piazza Belli, expressing our desire to fight for the right to life, was a duty to Giorgiana and ourselves, expressing not only our grief but also our determination in the struggle. But I felt isolated. I decided to take flowers to Giorgiana with two other sisters and then return to the meeting in my neighbourhood, because I thought it important to carry our message to the communities we live in.

29

I went in the local procession with that image of piazza Belli in my mind – empty but for a man arranging flowers in the only part of the square that wasn't taken over by cars.

The decision by the women, not to take on the political leadership of the processions and not to express any alternative message, weighed on the procession. I felt out of place and I'm sure that if more sisters had come it would have helped to create a greater sense of solidarity in the various districts of the city.

C.

Marginalised Baggio

I live in Baggio, a dormitory district of Milan, where working people stay home in the evening to get themselves together for another working day and the marginalised teenagers prostitute themselves or steal to pay for a 'trip' to death.

What is there at Baggio? Take your pick: a single cinema which puts on appalling films, bars with billiard tables and juke boxes full of the usual rubbishy 'top of the pops'.

Baggio also offers: moonlighting, real estate speculation and mafia pimps living on prostitution, gambling and shopkeepers' protection money, who stage shoot-outs in the street at night to settle accounts between themselves.

There are no social services at Baggio, the air is polluted by the fumes from a factory, there's very little green (a park next to the public library is littered with hypodermics left by junkies).

Eighteen per cent of the minors who end up in the Milan juvenile prison come from Baggio, and so did 5 out of the 16 heroin deaths registered in Milan during the last four years.

Heroin, mixed with lactose, strychnine, wallplaster etc., is sold at about 250,000 lire a gram to the 500 addicts round the neighbourhood. An addict therefore needs about ten million lire (£6,000) a month to pay for his habit. To find this money the addict turns to burglary, prostitution or pushing for the drug network which daily supplies about 400 grams of heroin to Baggio.

The only alternative place in Baggio is an abandoned building, occupied during the last two years by new left organisations. Neighbourhood people can meet there to discuss their problems and develop political and cultural activities (there's a library, courses on photography and music, and decent films are shown).

The ex-drug addicts participate actively in work for the centre and in the political initiatives, which offer them the human contact it's so hard to find.

Recently comrades from the centre have directly tackled the problem of heroin: a road-block with a huge cardboard syringe on the tram rails, leaflets distributed to local people who were somewhat surprised by this strange event, and on the same evening a sit-in at the public library where the health commission was meeting. Thanks to our intervention, the commission had to admit that in four years they hadn't managed to do anything real about the heroin problem.

Pushed by us, the commission said the problem existed on a vast scale and was impossible to solve as it would require an enormous amount of money to set up centres for addicts (though the local government has managed to find 500 million lire to re-build an old monastery, classified as a national monument but of no use to anyone as it's always closed).

Then we had a demonstration at the hospital where addicts wanting a cure often turn up at the emergency unit in a pitiful state and are regularly sent away – so they go back to stealing, get themselves arrested and end up in prison, where there's plenty of heroin and violence around to make their situation worse. We set up an exhibition outside the hospital showing sixty hypodermic syringes, all picked up in the park during a single morning, and we explained the drug situation at Baggio and our demands, to the administration, hospital 'barons', nurses and social workers.

We managed to interest the press and a national TV network in our campaign; let's hope this will serve to involve the parties of the conventional left, who have always ignored this problem. For example, the Communist Party appears at Baggio only to recruit members, pour venom on violence of any political colour, or to go on the annual demonstration with the DC on the anniversary of the Liberation.

So at Baggio, as everywhere else, the PCI divides the working class into two sides: on one hand the good workers who make sacrifices and respect the democratic institutions of the state, and

31

on the other, the youthful rebels who are violent, have nothing to say and (why not?) are into drugs.

To combat this line, we comrades at Baggio want our barracks to become an officially recognised social centre, with funds allocated, so that the district can at least offer an alternative to the present squalor.

Communist greetings,

Nicola

Francesco isn't here

Naples

It's like a nightmare: this morning the sun, comrades, the demonstration, now the loneliness of this room and Francesco in prison. All of this in ten hours – ten hours in which I've felt in succession anger, joy, hunger, waiting, sadness, fear and that terrible feeling of impotence.

An impotence which freezes the brain, which stops me from thinking or reasoning, because I'm losing the threads of the argument: how is it possible that Francesco was with us yesterday evening, laughing and playing the guitar, and now he's alone, in prison, beaten up and charged with possessing explosives? How can I imagine not seeing him, even for one day, not being able to talk to him or squeeze his hands? There's no explanation, no reason, nothing to justify his ending up in jail at the age of 25, our being robbed of a comrade's joy, anger and struggle, even for a few hours. No reason can explain why Francesco isn't here tonight, playing his guitar, cadging my cigarettes and chatting about this and that. No-one can justify the desperation I feel inside, having to stay alone in this room full of his things, having to say goodbye to him this evening, having to tell him I love him in a telegram to the prison. I still hope to wake up any moment and find it was all a nightmare and tomorrow Francesco will be coming here to do all the usual things: instead I have to get through this awful night alone and tomorrow face the telephone calls, the solicitor, trying to get news. It's absurd how bad you feel when they arrest someone you know well – it isn't selfishness, it's that when you read about the arrest of an unknown comrade, someone you've never seen,

32

even if you feel angry and bad it soon passes, because for you it's just a name and a photograph and you can be cool, you can reason and fight all the better. But when it's a comrade you've made love with, laughed with, whose every mannerism you are familiar with, then your head seems to shatter and you're left only with thousands of unanswerable questions, disconnected memories and a sense of emptiness and impotence. Even anger seems lost in the growing sadness, the helplessness, the need to cry. You can't even talk to the others because you don't know what to say.

Too much confusion, too much chaos in your head to work things out logically. Better stay here for a while waiting to be calm enough to think straight, finding consolation in a sheet of paper which will end up heaven knows where, expressing your thoughts, questions and pain.

Serenella

An American in Rome

Rome

I was very afraid the other day in Campo de'Fiori [at the 12 May demonstration attacked by the police] and that fear made me want to write this letter. I'm an Italo-American comrade (yes, from the States), and I came to Italy to study, to find my own roots, and because I rejected many aspects of American life and wanted to know if I'd be happier here. I still want to know.

In the USA I rejected my home town, so English-bourgeois, so 'white' and beautiful, where maybe only one black family lives, where other boys made me feel that my Italian origin was something inferior to be ashamed of.

I rejected imperialism, capitalism, big houses, big cars etc. I rejected all those people ignorant of the role of the USA plays in the world. I rejected the USA as the centre of my world and its power as the top nation. I hated the propaganda used by the politicians in the Italo-American communities against Italian communism. I rejected it and hated it.

The USA is still here around me and I still hate it. I hate the warships in the bay at Taormina, I hate the stories the American soldiers tell, repeated to me by Greek, Sardinian and Spanish

33

friends. I hate Coca-Cola, colour television, I hate the americanisation of this part of the world, the people's acceptance of American things.

And now, I reject Italy. I reject the lack of freedom, the police state. I was living in an illusion. I believed that the Italian people were ready to embrace communism – but that isn't so. I hear people talking on the bus, on the streets, in my building. I hear ignorance. They don't understand they're still living in a fascist state, all they hear is television propaganda. They want peace without liberty, they don't understand the meaning of violence. I think Italy is moving backwards.

I can't see much progress, much difference between the fascist republic and today. I'm convinced that to change Italy we'd have to evacuate most of the populace – they must be shown what things are like elsewhere. I know that the question of ignorance is deeper than that – we're talking about years spent under the influence of the Church and the Christian Democrats. The Italian mentality won't change so quickly.

The same thing can be said for the American mentality. Americans must consume less energy and have smaller cars and houses. But they've got the habit of seeing everything big and that won't change quickly.

I'm feeling very uncertain right now. I feel a terrible division, I'm like two people. I'm thinking about going back to the States, I'm not sure I want to stay in Italy. I don't want to live in a fascist state, a police state. I don't want to live in a country where it's so difficult to find work, to feel a useful member of society.

I'm sure going back to the States would be bad for me. I'd still reject it and with even more hatred. Perhaps I'm not mature enough to choose between two realities, American and Italian. Perhaps I'm looking for an island where I don't have to reject things any more.

Two things are certain: I love Italy, I want to go on living with my comrades. My friends all over the world tell me that the Italian comrades have given me a vitality I never had before. It's true, it's really true.

Greetings to all the comrades.

An American in Rome

34

Giorgiana

> ... if the October revolution
> > had been in May
> if you were still alive
> if I wasn't so helpless thinking about your murder
> if my pen was an invincible weapon
> if my fear exploded in the streets
> > courage born of strangled anger
> if having known you could be our strength
> if the flowers we gave to
> > your courageous life in our death
> > could become garlands
> > to the struggle of all of us, women
> if . . .
> > we wouldn't need words to affirm life
> > but life itself and nothing else.

The feminist comrades

The postscript of this letter refers to the policeman Antonio Custrà, shot dead during a demonstration in Milan. A fist raised with two fingers extended to imitate a gun was the gesture used by the Autonomists during demonstrations, instead of the classical clenched fist, and their chants praised the use of the P38 revolver.

Just like us

Three o'clock in the afternoon, my girlfriend's hand in mine, *Lotta Continua* in my pocket and a great anger inside, I set off to the rally, but something's upsetting me, and suddenly I realise. Two days ago Giorgiana and her bloke set out from home just like us, probably discussing the same sort of problems as us. They couldn't know that the murderous rage of authority would strike them, on a day supposed to be dedicated to peaceful struggle. Here we are again in the streets to shout that Giorgiana lives – not true, not true, not true, she's been cut to pieces in the mortuary.

The authorities have deliberately sought and found a new victim, as usual someone who had made a clear political choice,

35

who had chosen to dedicate her 19-year-old life to the movement, instead of the squalid indifference of so many. And this is inconvenient, very inconvenient for certain people.

No, Giorgiana, you're not alive, though we'll never forget you.

Bobo

PS. Because it has the sense of an attack against our movement, I condemn the murder of the policeman in Milan and call to all comrades of the revolutionary movement to take their distance from the P38 gun-slinging provocateurs.

From a notorious red school

Rome

The feminist comrades of the I Liceo Artistico in via Ripetta, the 'notorious red school', denounce the behaviour of their male 'comrades' who for some time have been boycotting and insulting us, showing their real sexist and fascist natures. Besides all the usual heavy macho repartee, these komrades have even said 'If you don't shut up, I'll smash your womb' (actual words of a komrade). They boycott our time together and have even thrown buckets of water over us while we were singing. When we protested they called us fascist and violent because we refused to turn the other cheek, and slogans appeared on all the walls, saying things like 'Feminist sucking cows' and worse – all signed with the hammer and sickle. The males even threw little notes out of the windows with obviously fascist phrases we find too offensive to repeat.

It should be noted that these male komrades call themselves 'feminists' and think they have the right to judge us. A typical remark is, 'You are false feminists', showing their desire to divide us and their annoyance at our ability to organise ourselves and come to decisions without their help.

We have reported these things, not because they are new to the feminist movement, but because they show that even in a school like ours where 'much has been said and much has been done' (including the pseudo-feminist theatre put on by the komrades), where fascists don't (or aren't supposed to) exist, an

36

appalling degree of repression and sexism exists among the komrades. It's yet another example of lack of self-criticism and unpreparedness for any discussion not based on insults and paternalism.

The feminist comrades of the I Liceo Artistico of via Ripetta

This letter refers to the events in Rome on 12 May, when the police attacked the Radicals' sit-in in piazza Navona.

To Silvio

Rome

Please publish this letter so that I can get in touch with a comrade who was with me in piazza Navona yesterday, until I lost sight of him when the police opened fire.

Silvio, I'd like to see you again, maybe on some other demonstration. I'd like to know what happened to you after we separated when the police blocked the exits. I got smashed on the head by one of the SPGs who was beating up everybody in sight.

I saw a lot of people looking for their friends or trying to get away. I saw a lot of blood and I cried, partly because of the tear gas canisters exploding everywhere, partly because I couldn't do anything – I couldn't go forward and I couldn't go back – and I cried because I was on my own and it was the first time I'd found myself mixed up in this sort of chaos, I cried for all the comrades running around wounded or lying on the ground, I cried because I couldn't do anything for them and I also cried because that sonofabitch Cossiga lost me a nice friend.

I'd gone to piazza Navona with my hair in plaits and a sweater tied over my shoulders to celebrate a great victory, to be with my comrades and have a good time, and instead the police ruined everything (and goddamit I didn't even have my plimsolls on). At school today we talked about yesterday's clashes with the police, but there weren't many of us at the meeting. At the Liceo Artistico there's never much support for these things.

Lots of them couldn't care less.

I've talked about things which have nothing to do with where

37

I started from, but at least I've got it off my chest. And now, to come back to us, I'd like to make a sort of appeal to you, Silvio, who I met on the 64 bus. If you happen to be in Rome, come and see me at school, at 11.50 when there's a break, or at 1.45 p.m. when we come out (the address is via Lungro 1, Quarto Miglio).

My thanks to *Lotta Continua,* Ciao,

Cinzia, a Radical Party comrade

At the Rimini Congress of Lotta Continua held in November 1976, the leaders of the party, challenged head on by the feminists, recognised their political failure and declared that they would no longer lead, but trust to the 'radicality of the movement'. Lotta Continua was thus in practice dissolved as a national body because the local offices had no national centre to refer to.

A halt to apathy

Turin

Dear comrades,
I want to comment on the letter from the Turin factory worker.

I've been an LC sympathiser for seven years and I've participated actively in a lot of struggles, or rather as many as circumstances allowed, at school, in the barracks. So, like many other comrades, I've had moments of crisis and disappointment, of excitement and joy. Frankly I've never understood 'militancy' as it was always defined until shortly before the Rimini Conference, and this often prevented me from attending the branch meeting more regularly. I found it oppressive and castrating, a solemn place for political talk, where the personal was kept for afterwards, and even then didn't exist. I never managed to start a decent relationship with anyone – faced with the 'total' or 'consistent' activist I became inarticulate or withdrawn. I've always done political work by including the personal, trying to be first a friend and then an activist, and I think I can say without conceit that this has borne excellent results in very different situations. I realised I was growing together with the people I talked to, who were often

38

put off by those who tried to lead 'from above', as the 'recognised vanguard'.

Given all this, the pre-congress period was very intense for me, though the atmosphere was often white-hot and oppressive, full of terrible fights and head-on clashes for absolutely sterile reasons and, let's face it, power games. Anyway, I felt a new wind blowing from somewhere and this gave me new strength and a great longing to understand, to start everything afresh, everyone together. For the first time I really felt part of what was happening. In this sense Rimini didn't disappoint me, and I think it represented and still represents something extremely important, an experience we must use. Everything that happened afterwards was a logical consequence, and it's right it should have happened.

But what now?

Now I'm in the same situation as that worker comrade, I don't understand a bloody thing, communicating has become really difficult again, I can't understand certain comrades now. Yesterday they were 'total' militants, today they're not militants, not total, not anything any more!

The wave of the crisis has washed us up on a shore which may not lead anywhere new. The comrades have rediscovered life – that's good, I'd even say it was time, but does the re-appropriation of life mean giving up the political?

Today everyone is into football matches, flowers for their girlfriends, rediscovering the poetry of Prévert. Yesterday has become shit. Some people even play at being Indians or freaks, some smoke joints, all depending on how you feel when you get up in the morning.

The Proletarian clubs [autonomous local organisations of 'marginalised' youth] threaten to become, if they aren't already, new party HQs, places where people talk and discuss in a different way, understand things and grow, but where the really marginalised – the unemployed, the drug addicts – are excluded again. The words 'Lotta Continua', 'party', 'organisation' have become taboo, if you use them you get jumped on and accused of conservative extremism, because 'you're an old-style comrade and we're in a new phase now'.

Well, comrades, I don't accept these conditions myself, I don't like this game, and anyway let's not forget that certain other

39

people aren't playing a game at all, so we're in danger of taking a leap in the dark which will set us back years and lose us all the gains we've made.

Like it or not, most of us spend our lives, eight or nine hours a day, at our workplace – isn't this our reality? So what do we say to our workmates who now more than ever see us as the only people capable of opposing the DC-PCI government, the only people capable of giving a lead? I feel these problems too, and I want to deal with the issue for my own sake and for others. It's convenient to 'dissolve' the party into the movement, but it doesn't help the movement to grow, it becomes suffocated. I believe we should look to the movement to try to develop a political project which would return to the movement and be tested there. It's time to call a halt to apathy: the years of struggle and experiences like Rimini mean we can do it.

Claudio C.

Blasted art!

Bari

I'm a 23-year-old comrade in my last year at the art college in Bari. My convictions and previous experience make me reject the art gallery as a way of communicating my works. I feel disorientated because I don't understand the role comrades like myself should play in this society, or in a future communist one. I don't agree with neo-realism, I believe in abstract painting – otherwise you end up in the Communist Party which tells you how to paint. I can't find an answer to all this. The lectures on the subject by intellectuals don't interest me. I want to find a way forward with others like myself, who have the same problems.

I therefore appeal to all interested comrades to contact me and open a debate in the paper.

I believe it wouldn't be a bad thing to talk about this blasted art and what we should do about it, and about those who make a living from it (I mean art as a service for the rich).

Communist greetings,

Pino Spadavecchia

Messina (Sicily) is the city with the highest concentration of fascist sympathisers in Italy.

Too much talk

Messina

My name is Vittoria, I'm a comrade from Messina. At 16 I'm already tired of struggle, resigned, especially now when I see how they kill us, taking away our right to demonstrate. I read in our paper (the only one which tells us what is really happening), about what happened at Rome, the death of comrade Giorgiana, the new police tactics. Comrades, it's sad to admit it, but it's how it is: they're smashing us, we're not going to win! You say we should collect petitions and demonstrate in the other cities as it can't be done in Rome any more. Two weeks ago in Messina the comrades of the Radical Party collected signatures, sold papers, distributed leaflets, but it lasted only two days.

Here we talk a lot, but we don't get down to any serious action. Here political work means standing around from 12.20 to 1.15 in front of the school, the fascists with their shiny boots and big motor bikes on one side, the comrades on the other, with *Lotta Continua* or *Il Manifesto* in their hands, asking the same old questions, organising meeting after meeting. We go on like this week after week until one day a fascist crosses over to the pavement the comrades are on, then another, then another, until thirty or forty of them are there to beat up the four comrades (always the same ones) who stayed around . . .

Recently the situation has been getting worse – there are groups of fascists walking the streets, some of them from other cities (particularly in the north) and usually we do nothing about it. Or rather we do do something – talk and talk and talk. When notorious fascist MPs come down, we do nothing. We welcome them with open arms instead of with stones, we go on talking and acting the intellectual in the assemblies. This is the situation in Messina, it's sad, as you can see.

When I hear about what's happening in Rome and in the other big cities and I compare it with what's happening, or rather not happening in Messina, I get angry enough to smash everything

41

in sight, but I also feel sad and resigned because I'm alone, because there are so few of us and we do nothing more than talk.

With a clenched fist,

Vittoria

Sante Notarnicola is considered the first of the 'communist political prisoners', who by 1979 officially numbered over a thousand in Italy. On 25 September 1967 he took part in an armed bank robbery in which 4 bystanders were killed and 25 wounded. He was given a life sentence.

In jail, Notarnicola wrote an autobiography (L'evasione impossibile) *describing how, as an ex-member of the Communist Party, he had been duped by his accomplices into believing that they were financing revolutionary political activity with the proceeds of their robberies. In the same book Notarnicola presented a theory about the revolutionary potential of the prison population. (A similar theory was behind the creation of the NAP – Armed Proletarian Nuclei – an armed terrorist group which, when it was active, was made up mainly of ex-prisoners.)*

In 1979 Notarnicola published a book of poetry.

For Francesco Lorusso

> A communist is dead,
> a communist is dead.
> Tie up the bells,
> flags
> at half-mast.
> Children, don't cry,
> bring red flowers from the fields,
> few words
> and no rhetoric,
> we know what is lost
> when a communist dies.

Sante Notarnicola

Activity in small towns

Seggiano (Milan)

Around Milan there are no ghetto districts because all the small towns are dormitories. A few 'oases' built for the middle class outside the city are quite separate and easily distinguishable (San Felice, Milano Due).

There are a lot of problems specific to these areas, beginning with commuting, by which the employers rob us of a few more hours of life and send us home ready for bed; there's a total lack of meeting places for young people, only the parish youth clubs and bars; there are hundreds of little 'family' manufacturers who exploit an enormous number of under-age workers; there's the problem of meeting up with young people in other places because of the almost complete lack of 'non-radial' transport; and in the most distant and isolated villages the priests still reign. But so as not to make a 'list' of problems, I'll start with one of the most deeply felt needs – a place to meet.

Here at Seggiano the only existing place is the parish youth club where, since 1968, the comrades have been coming for meetings, where political initiatives begin and lots of young people come to be together and enjoy themselves, where the neighbourhood action committee meets and where all the cultural grass roots organisations have been born, died and re-born. It's been the headquarters for the collection of electricity and telephone bills in the 'self-reduction' campaigns, for popular festivals, theatre and pop music.

However, this facility naturally has its limits, being a religious establishment, and every once in a while the two democratic priests get sermons and threats from on high. So we decided to take over another building which could be completely self-managed by the youth and local people.

A young workers' club was set up here in the wake of the Milan collectives. It was meant as a social centre, but because the specific needs and problems of the area hadn't been seriously discussed and because it tried to do things as they were done in Milan, it was dissolved after a few months. In fact, although it's right to participate in general struggles, it's also right to build

43

everything up starting from where you live, and this is another problem for the provinces . . .

Thanks to the experience of comrades who lived through the 'crisis of militancy' and the 'new approach to politics', with the refusal to follow blindly the ideas of the 'big shots' from Milan, as happened in the past, contact has been built up with many more young people; sport is now seen as an area for political action and a universal need, many more people participate in building up an alternative culture, etc.

Naturally, not everything goes smoothly. There are contradictions, limitations, things we'd like to do and don't. This is an invitation to all comrades to discuss the specific problems of the provinces, with a view to organising political activity in the small towns.

Viviana

Some reasons for discontent

Venice

I'm a worker at Petrolchimico, Marghera. In ten years there I've always been elected onto the factory council and I'm quite well known both for the part I've played in the council and general assemblies, and as an activist in LC which I've supported since 1969, though recently in a very peripheral way.

The questions I want to bring up are so complex that I can only touch on them, but I hope I'll be able to make myself understood and start some debate.

The factory workers – and workers in general – have completely lost faith in the traditional institutions and organisations, not because they realise that the 'bourgeois state must be overthrown and can't be reformed', but simply because they're tired of being fucked about. For example, since 1970 the unions have been putting forward 'political' demands, starting with reforms and the 'new way of producing cars', and ending with industrial diversification and full employment. At a rank and file level these demands have been supported by struggles which have sometimes been tough and exciting, because the workers wanted it that way, but the higher up the level of negotiation (regional,

44

national, etc.) the more the struggle has been diluted. The end of this process being the national 'victories'.

The workers' reply to these sell-outs, especially after the latest and biggest cons, has been formal or at the most partial.

Every day our paper reports on various struggles and explains that those striking etc. have understood everything, that is, the final aim of their struggle and the general context their particular confrontation fits into. The trouble is that invariably the union or party rips them off; but why do the workers go on getting ripped off if they've understood everything? It's often said that it's because there's no credible alternative, no efficient national organisation, no definite and consistent reference point. The leading sections have always thought their role was to propose better objectives or call meetings to organise a harder struggle – meanwhile in the social arena, certain sections belonging to or identifying with the working class have shattered traditional concepts of struggle and now are important expressions of the movement, i.e. – the organised unemployed;

the women's movement;

the current generation of students.

These people have drastically challenged the traditional way of relating to organisations – at least in some respects. Starting from what is positive in their experience, we must have the courage to say no to the union-led strikes, particularly inside the factory. I'll try to clarify.

Take for example the strike of 27 April, the four-hour strike in the big companies, when the workers, in greater numbers than ever before – 60 per cent – stayed at home on holiday or sick, not because they were scabs, but simply because they didn't want to lose four hours' pay for nothing. (This has lately become a habit for Petrolchimico – they call it 'voluntary lay-off'.)

In consequence we get more and more opportunists, that is people who say 'by striking I lose money, by going on holiday at least I get the four hours.'

There is a political reality behind this which they sense intuitively, even if they can't give it a shape and consequently a proper answer. It's no use struggling in this way for industrial renewal, full employment and a healthier environment, as the employers will never fully concede what we want; at the most they'll

45

give us what they can get back later. To defeat the boss and his political minions we need a frontal and generalised confrontation.

I'll give another example, when the union claims a victory has been gained with the agreement on wage costs, this is pure shit for two reasons:
1) if someone wants to cut off my balls and I persuade him to cut off only one it doesn't mean I've won a victory;
2) the employers say that the wage costs affect the competitiveness of the product, but individual productivity also affects competitiveness. And everyone knows that not only has there been an increase in overall production and a decrease of the labour force, giving greater productivity, but that the main objectives of the bosses are to eliminate loss-making production and increase moonlighting, natural wastage and sackings.

Now, on these questions either we can just get indignant, or we can organise a protest which doesn't substantially change anything, or we can try to get a clean break, refusing the union strikes which have the sole aim of passing off the needs of capital as working-class victories.

To finish with, I'd like to talk about LC for a moment. I've been a convinced Lotta Continua activist right from the beginning, then as the struggles came and went I realised that it's not enough to be the angriest, the leader of strikes for half an hour off the working week, for fifty- instead of twenty-thousand lire more. People want to hear from us what 'power to the masses' means, what an all-out struggle against the employers would mean for them. The fact is we haven't understood that most of the working class feel they have gone from 0 to 100; for us their 100 is 0, so we're convinced it still is for them too. We have to accept their fears about 'extremists' and discuss these with them, without thinking that a new aim will be enough to organise them. We must explain clearly that real violence isn't generated by the revolutionaries but by the bosses, through exploitation, unemployment, fatal accidents at work, discrimination, the lack of social services, division between old and young and inequality between the sexes – that capitalist society is in fact the essence of violence and that, anyway, their 100 has already gone down to 50.

Communist greetings,

Beppe

Otherwise it will be useless

Rome

This letter is prompted by the need to express my disappointment and anger following the mass meeting held in via del Governo Vecchio on Saturday, in the hope that it will open a calmer debate amongst women comrades. It's very difficult to attempt to express one's own ideas in this moment of enormous confusion. I was very angry on Saturday coming out of via del Governo Vecchio after a violent meeting which expressed only aggressiveness, and no ability to create real dialogue and understanding, no realisation that the question, once again, is the problem of the relation between 'feminist' and 'political' issues (by which I mean those struggles which are not ours alone, but are common to all comrades).

This incapacity to talk to one another, to accept one another, derives from the false division between 'feminists' and 'women comrades' which ignores the fact that being a feminist necessarily means being a comrade, because we're all struggling against an oppressive society which takes away life, which doesn't supply adequate structures, which relegates us to a subordinate role. At this moment we must realise that to struggle against Cossiga and the new police authority doesn't mean denying our struggle as feminists. It means claiming a place in this society, claiming *our* right to struggle, since none of us passively follow our male comrades onto the streets – we do it freely as feminists, as comrades. If we don't understand that in each one of us there is, and must be, a comrade and a feminist, if we don't understand that our struggle must be directed to the outside, to claim freedoms they deny us, if we allow ourselves to be 'ghettoised' again, this time in the [state-supported] neighbourhood clinics, we'll end up being permanently excluded from a part of reality that they – the government, the comrades, the men – will continue to run, often on our backs . . .

Giorgiana's death is that of a feminist comrade, killed while she was struggling for her right to expression, for her existence in conflict with this society: we must carry on her struggle or her death will have been useless.

Silvia

47

The bicycle

Milan

On Saturday 14 March, while I was following the demonstration along via Torino on my push bike, a comrade marching behind the LC banner asked to borrow my bike to get up to the front quickly. I lent it to him, but I haven't seen it since.

I hope it's all a mix-up – so I ask this comrade to return the bike to me at the central branch office as soon as possible. Otherwise I'll have to think I'm the biggest fool in town.

Marco

The main issue for the New Left in Italy in the 70s was the practice of militant anti-fascism, in which the extra-parliamentarians claimed to be continuing the glorious tradition of the Resistance movement of 1943-45. Together with a fringe of militant ex-partisans, they defined the Resistance as an experience of revolutionary class struggle deliberately 'betrayed' and politically mystified during the following years, as the Communist Party moved towards social-democratic positions. The PCI, the leading force in the historical armed struggle, insisted that the Resistance had been essentially national in character, aimed at ridding Italy of the German invaders rather than preparing a revolution; all progressive forces in Italy, including the Christian Democrats, had collaborated harmoniously to this end.

The young militants marched in the streets to the old partisan songs and slogans like 'The Resistance is red, it isn't Demochristian', and 'We are the new partisans.' Round this theme a dialogue with the elder generation of the PCI rank and file became possible, and some veterans relegated to the margins of the party found a new role as figureheads in neo-stalinist organisations. The first clandestine armed groups formed after 1970 also claimed to be continuing the Resistance, borrowing or adapting the old names (GAP, Red Brigades). How to interpret the Resistance and its relation to the revolutionary left today ('Why are the partisan terrorists of 1943–45 considered heroes and the terrorists of today criminals?') remained an unsolved question. But after 1977 it was sometimes suggested that the uncritical acceptance of an ideal of armed violent struggle, in

48

previous years, was one reason for its spread at the end of the decade.

Like a tramp

Casalpusterlengo (Milan)

Comrades,

I'm writing to you about the miserable death of a comrade. Last week Aristide Grossi, 55 years old, partisan, was found dead near a little country church on the road to Mulino Magnani. He had taken an overdose of barbiturates.

The place he went to die is nick-named by the locals 'Lazzaretto' (leper hospital). Perhaps Aristide didn't choose it by accident.

For a long time he'd been outside the circle of comrades and friends he had fought alongside in the Resistance. After the Liberation he had a series of raw deals and strokes of bad luck that reduced him to a precarious, poverty-stricken condition. And he was more and more alone in his troubles. After the great collective experience of the Resistance (he really fought and risked his life, in the GAP [urban 'terrorist' groups], and a lot of partisans still remember him today) he felt perhaps more than others the betrayal of the communist ideal.

Convinced that 'we have to carry on the struggle', he didn't know how to cope with his personal problems. He had seen too many 'comrades' taking advantage of their heroic reputation (particularly those who, unlike him, never risked much, and waited for the right moment). Recently he had become a chronic alcoholic and was practically a tramp, in and out of hospitals and homes. Then he just wanted to die.

This is already a dreadful story, demonstrating once again the truth that for many of us the Resistance was betrayed, and through this betrayal a whole generation of dedicated communists was sacrificed and destroyed, thrown away by the 'political leaders'.

But I haven't written just to say this. After the tragedy of his suicide, I've had to watch the macabre farce of the end of this story. Of course Aristide Grossi had a pauper's funeral. The 'red'

49

council of Codogno put up funeral notices which weren't signed and didn't even mention his history – as they do for tramps, in fact. Not only this, but not one anti-fascist party – and today there are so many, too many – thought of sending a flag or a delegation. Only the PCI deputy mayor came to the funeral in his personal capacity. There was no trace of ANPI [National Association of Italian Partisans], although Aristide had his membership card in his pocket when he died. The president of ANPI, who was in the Resistance with Aristide, was nowhere to be seen. Later I asked him why he hadn't been there and why there'd been no poster, no flag, and he replied that he had sent a wreath 'costing 70,000 lire' – anonymous, however.

So Aristide was buried like a pauper. His past had already been buried long ago by these so-called communists and democrats – ever since when, instead of choosing him, an active working-class communist, they chose the 'middle classes', the 'entrepreneurs' and the Christian Democrats, the priests and the policemen of this 'democratic' state.

I've written to say, comrades, that Aristide is not anonymous, he's one of *our* dead.

But I've also written to let these new 'gentlemen' (who are just like the old ones) know that even if they've conned and swindled Aristide, they won't be able to do it to all of us. There are still people of my generation who haven't been disarmed. And they don't intend to be, in the face of no matter what 'compromise'.

Luigi Croce, 'Bill', partisan commander

Adele Faccio, a Radical Party member, proposed a pro-abortion law in parliament. During the debate she was called an 'ugly cow' and other sexist abuse.

Beautiful and ugly

Monte Sant' Angelo

In the paper of 26 May there's an article entitled 'The fascist Pecorino's little dog', with the phrase, 'Besides the anger a woman feels when she sees these squalid, *ugly, fat* men who decide on

50

something so important to our lives . . .' There can be no doubt that these words refer explicitly to the physical appearance of the senators. Anyway, comrades, I don't believe your rage would have been any less if instead of 'ugly, fat' senators they had been 'handsome, lithe and athletic' like Alain Delon.

I'd like to point out that this sort of dismissive comment on a person's physical appearance is typically fascist (or nazi). You should bear in mind how comrade Adele Faccio was insulted by fascist and Christian-Democrat deputies (and maybe others) during the debate on abortion.

Excuse me for taking it so seriously, but I believe this isn't just a casual slip – there's a whole (bourgeois and fascist) ideology behind it which exists in comrades too. It's not only the style of referring to a person's physical appearance that I want to criticise, it's the whole idea of 'beautiful' and 'ugly' which we all have to some extent. There are a great many comrades who avoid, or at best put up with 'ugly' women comrades, and the same goes for women comrades. Undoubtedly these comrades have their own conceptions of beautiful and ugly which elicit from them a response of attraction to the beautiful, and of repulsion from the ugly.

When it's pointed out to them that today we have conceptions or models of 'beautiful' and 'ugly' which are imposed on us by the bourgeoisie, they reply, 'There is no beauty as such' – since they agree that there is no universal conception of beauty – 'but beauty is in the eye of the beholder', as if our vision is absolutely our own, rather than something imposed from outside in a lifelong process of assimilation.

I don't want to go on at greater length. But I think these things should be taken up in the paper and amongst comrades, if we really want to change our way of being revolutionaries.

I hope this letter can be a starting point for such a debate.

Communist greetings,

L.G.

The 'Lockheed scandal' broke in 1976, after US sources published evidence that large bribes had been paid to Italian ministers to secure orders for military aircraft. Two ex-ministers were retired and things were smoothed over. The Communist Party agreed that state financing of political parties was the way to avoid future corruption, and a bill providing for this was quickly passed.

For a pair of jeans

Palermo

Dear comrades,
You will have noticed the health campaign launched by the press, with the *Corriere della Sera* in the lead, against tight jeans.

Suddenly journalists and scientists, gynaecologists and geneticists have realised that jeans cause eczema, dermatitis, orchitis, vaginitis, male and female sterility. Is this a flowering of humanity in our men of science, at last concerned about the health of young workers in blue jeans?

Not at all. It's a campaign to launch a new fashion – wide jeans – which the fashion manufacturers have been planning for about two years, reaching us slightly later than the rest of Europe! The system used is the same as for Lockheed aircraft, only selling Hercules C130 means greasing the palms of presidents and ministers while opening the market for wide jeans means paying only a few 'experts'.

Mario Sala

When a worker dies

Bari

When a policeman dies it goes on the front pages of all the papers with lots of pictures, but when a worker dies the press (when it puts it in at all) gives it a couple of lines. Are there first-rate and second-rate deaths? We're a group of metalworkers in a Bari factory, and we demand that every time a worker dies on the job the press give it wide coverage. If the papers were full of news about the death of workers, what would it mean? What would it do to public opinion? Our lives are hard too, we too leave everything for ever, this earth, our loved ones: and we have the most vital of tasks, the production of wealth for a country which doesn't deserve it, because in the end all we get in exchange is injustice, sacrifice, violent death and indifference.

19 signatures

Exorcism

Mestre (Venice)

Dear Editor,
I'm a 17-year-old boy. I've been very shocked by something which has happened to my brother, who is 23 and has been defined by competent people as a schizophrenic. After hearing from the doctors that nothing could be done to make him normal again, my parents applied to a priest with a reputation for healing the incurable. The priest explained my brother's strange behaviour by saying he was possessed by the devil and the only remedy, as in ancient days, was exorcism.

Since this priest was very young, he didn't feel ready to rid a human body of the devil, so he advised going to a priest capable of doing it.

Luckily my parents realised how absurd this procedure was and gave it up.

The fact remains that in a so-called civilised country, mentally sick patients have to submit to every sort of violence from the healthy part of society.

Please don't publish my name.

PS. I'm enclosing a copy of the prayers supposed to cure schizophrenia.

Experience in an institute for handicapped people

Comrades,
I feel the need to campaign, especially when I think of those ghettoes they call boarding institutes where I've lived for years, I want to struggle against the system of exploitation we handicapped have to submit to.

Having an institutional experience I know how we handicapped are kept apart from what's *really* going on in the country,

53

or rather how they only let us see the things they want us to – we are used, especially by the clergy, as most institutes are controlled by nuns and priests. However, in many institutes the young people have got rid of the nuns, this happens where the kids are more grown up and have gained a consciousness of the world around them and have rebelled against it. But even if the nuns have gone there are still the priests or the director and his assistants – nothing has changed, we're still exploited and this can be changed only if all the exploited (workers, housewives, the handicapped etc.) unite and fight against this system, which is really good only at exploiting (and accepting bribes).

Iosella

Asinara is a small island off Sardinia where an old prison has been converted into a high security jail. Four other penal institutes of this sort, reserved for 'dangerous prisoners', were set up after a series of spectacular jail breaks by BR and NAP fighters. Asinara is extremely difficult for visitors to reach, and the regime in the prison is particularly harsh.

Asinara – my home

Cesena

Dear comrades of the editorial staff,
The letters page is very good and interesting, sometimes more so than certain leading articles. I get the feeling of talking, listening, communicating with lots of comrades who often have the same problems as me, so there's a sense of friendship with people I've never met.

I'm writing to you (I've never done it before) because I wanted to raise a question – not only for the editors but all comrades in LC – about the problem of prisons.

The only letters from prisons are from comrades recently arrested in Rome, Bologna, etc., but a great many workers and comrades inside would like to write and communicate with the comrades outside.

54

I've been inside. For six months in Gaeta military prison, from March to September 1972. The paper wrote about it (briefly).

Anyway, this (forced) experience taught me a lot, in particular it allowed me to see for myself what conditions in prison are like.

I don't want to talk about myself but about a dear friend and comrade whom I knew inside, whom I shared food with. Now years later I've heard from him again. He's still in prison. He needs help badly, he needs friendship and love (yes, really – true love, feeling, humanity).

I don't want to go on about it or ask for your pity. I'd like you to publish the enclosed letter from him. I hope a great many comrades, men and women and particularly Sardinians, will give him support. I also hope his letter will open a debate on the question of prisons, on internal and external intervention (see *The Wretched of the Earth* [by Frantz Fanon]) and give proletarians in jail an alternative to the suicidal and isolated prospect of the NAP or BR. Many people inside see NAP or BR as the normal choice in the struggle against the bourgeois state.

Is there a 'new way of being political' inside the prisons as well, or are we interested only in students, workers etc., and the issues imposed on us by the regime?

OK, do as you like, I've gone on too long, you can cut my letter, there were a lot of things I wanted to say. But please publish Paolo's letter.

Ciao,

Fabrizio

From Paolo Schirru, Asinara Prison

Dear Fabrizio,

First of all, please excuse my long silence. But you'll understand it isn't my fault, it's the fault of those pigs who wouldn't let me write to anyone except my parents, and who held me in solitary confinement for nearly a year – you've probably heard that I had a little difference of opinion with two of those fascist vermin because I'd come to the defence of a comrade they were picking on and beating up; one day they pulled out knives and were going to slash him, I saw red and jumped on them, making them drop the knives,

55

then I beat them both up. I thought they wouldn't try it on again with me or the other comrade, but three days later when I was going to the bathroom to wash some things they came up behind me and knifed me *three* times, then they ran away and got themselves transferred to another prison so I couldn't get at them.

Anyway, I must be boring you so I'll change the subject and talk about us. I'm back in this god-forsaken island Asinara, I'm in good health, as I hope with all my heart are you, your wife and your little boy Simone.

As you know, Fabrizio, I've been so many years rotting here between these god-forsaken walls, sometimes I lose my mind and think of ending it all, then I think: why shouldn't I have the same strength and will power as others who've been here longer, to stick it out to the end? Then I relax and think and day-dream of the day I'll see the liberty I've been waiting for for so long, though it can't be called freedom any more outside these walls, with everything that's happening. Anyway, it's still better to be outside, then at least I'll be able to fight by your side really, instead of just with my thoughts and my proletarian consciousness.

You don't know how often I dream of being outside, alongside the comrades, but '79 is still a long way away, and my anger just accumulates inside me. I don't speak to anyone here, because you risk ending up in solitary and I've got to be careful because I've spent enough time there and I couldn't take any more.

Listen, Fabrizio, I feel very alone, try to give me support, I can't go on any more. Once you asked me if I wanted to correspond with a girl, well, yes, I would – I so much need someone to break through my solitude and all the sadness around me.

I want to say a lot more, but at the moment I can't, you'll understand why . . .

Now I'll end with a fraternal hug to you and your family and a big kiss to Simone.

Ciao – *Freedom*,

Paolo

God created hell, then not content he created Asinara . . .
56

PS. – Looking forward to a letter from you.
Ciao,

Paolo

She became a comrade

Rome

I'm a boy of 20, a friend of Isabella Pelloni, a real friend from early adolescence, when we see everything with purer eyes, there's less poison inside us, and we can still be interested in the sun and a beautiful blue sky. She was my friend for a long, extraordinary summer, a summer of long talks, lively discussions and real communication. But as it was born, everything came to an end or, to be honest, was repressed.

We went our separate ways, two different roads which meant an end to our friendship, which in fact set us against each other. I, drawn into a certain sort of world, took up the squalid career of a fascist. She became a comrade and a revolutionary. Now her death has made me understand a lot. I've realised that perhaps I could have done something to help save her, beyond the ideological barrier, that instead of deliberately forgetting her telephone number out of stupid, useless pride, I should have rung it several times a day, if only to let her know I was there, to tell her of my new longing to destroy this system of materialistic life in which the individual, destroyed by the daily struggle to survive, tends constantly to improvement, but in a subjective rather than collective sense, thus becoming aggressive and hateful. Isabella needed me too, that awful Sunday of 22 May when she turned on the gas and finished with this treacherous, shitty life we all hate, because it's an eternal compromise, an eternal not being yourself, an eternal denial, it's not being able to shout with joy in a full bus because you'd get locked up in an asylum, it's not being able to shout with pain and sadness in a bar crowded with people reduced to robots because they wouldn't understand you. But we all have the same problems, the same existential crisis; despite this we go on ignoring each other and carrying on as if nothing was wrong, as if the sacrifice of Isabella's life and of so many others was in vain.

Let's try and learn something from them. Now Isabella isn't

57

here anymore, I understand how much I needed her, now I feel like I can't go on any more, now I'm trying to summon up the courage to imitate her gesture, I understand how important it is that young people unite as one and struggle together warmly and in one blood, as friends.

Paolo

Poetry, lots of poetry

Milan

Poetry for Francesco Lorusso, poetry for Giorgiana (a full notebook from Rome), poetry on the movement, on us, on everything: now coming out in *Lotta Continua* and other publications, or in duplicated sheets and other mysterious underground means of communication. It seems the comrades' interest in this new form of expression is growing. Shamefully hidden in wardrobes, or at the back of drawers under dusty packages of leaflets, read furtively in the depths of night behind locked doors with tiny groups of fellow conspirators, linked almost by a blood pact, poems have come back to flower in this saddest of springs, one would think the least suitable time for something so subtle and sophisticated, something so detached from reality, from mass struggle, from politics. And then – poetry is the prerogative of intellectuals, of sighing languid souls, of girls in love, sometimes of militant comrades but only when off duty; this juvenile habit should not – heaven preserve us – interfere with their public image as leaders. After all the masses don't like poetry, they don't understand it, you can't go to the factory at six o'clock in the morning and give a worker a poem, he'd be furious; and if the poetry talks about how you feel when you're with a woman, or walking through the streets, or what passes through your mind, or suggests a magnificent sunset (polluted) or worse, goes on about all those (petty-bourgeois) paranoias and pessimisms, then he gets twice as furious (these workers, you know . . .) At the outside (at the very outside, however) he can accept a poem on contracts and negotiations, perhaps on Kossiga, written in simple words with the masses (rhymed with classes) the struggle (hard) and lots of red flags.

58

But who says it's really like this? Can't poetry be a way to freedom and re-birth? A way of discovering a new language, a new way of communicating with yourself and with others? A road to liberation, to freedom, of creation and imagination?

Is it harder to understand a poem than an editorial? Is it pleasanter in the early morning, on an empty stomach, to read a poem, or a heavy leaflet on the political situation in Italy in the light of recent events putting forward a perspective towards a global view, but considering the previous facts which puts us, all things taken into consideration, and without neglecting previously stated principles, in a position to formulate a complex strategy? Is the poetry of a young girl in love more languid than the confessions of an ex-galactic mega-leader thrown into confusion by the Rimini Conference?

All comrades who have written/write poetry/stories, who want to discuss, create, read, improvise or at least understand what it's all about (we ourselves understand very little) who want to take poetry out from where it's been kept (Freedom for poetry!) should contact us.

We want to publish (in a simple form, of course) all the poems we can find, give them around, read them everywhere (or where we can), improvise them, put them on the walls etc. And see what happens.

We're sure of one thing: Kossiga doesn't write poetry (how could he?)

Francesco, Lucio, Claudio

From Maria, for Vittoria

Motta Camastra (Messina)

Dear comrades,
In the paper (24 May) I read the letter from comrade Vittoria from Messina about the bad situation in her city, about the fact that there are very few of us who want to change this filthy society. I'm 16 years old and I live in a village in the province of Messina, a place where things are really going badly: out of ten young people here, six couldn't care less (i.e. are DC), two are fascists and two say they are on the left (the old left, of course). I'm in Lotta

Continua and my brother is Radical Party. This is the situation in my village (900 inhabitants) which I have to face every day, I generally come out defeated because, like Vittoria, I'm alone. Then I get furious too and would like to smash everything in sight, but I don't feel resigned (I don't think I shall even at 80), and I want to go on fighting. At my school (technical institute of commerce) there are communist slogans on the wall but that's about all.

I'd be pleased if Vittoria contacted me since we don't live very far apart, perhaps she could start by writing to me, so please publish this letter with my address.

With a clenched fist,

Maria Catena

The dear nuns

Rome

Dear comrades,

I'd like to tell you about what seems to me to be a very serious thing, which happened in a hostel run by nuns in via Palestro 23-25. This is one of many hostels in Rome where foreigners and girls from the south (like myself) can stay whilst waiting to find domestic work with a 'highclass' bourgeois family. The sisters chose the right afternoon, I don't remember if it was Thursday or Sunday (the days when the boarders have a half day off). I couldn't have cared less about the 'very interesting' film (according to the good sisters) that they were going to show about abortion. I wanted to have my supper quickly and get out. However, a nun stopped me at the kitchen door saying supper would be served later (not true at all – when I went to the kitchen after the film they had already put everything away – but by that time I wasn't feeling hungry, anyway, after what they'd practically forced me to see). The film consisted of a series of arranged stills which the great horror-film-makers would have envied. I saw incredible things, babies cut into pieces and put in plastic bags, mincers for human flesh (according to the priest who commented with a voice quivering with hate) where the nurses threw screaming foetuses because the noise irritated them, bloody creatures emerging with an arm or even the

60

head pulled off during the abortion, and similar horrors. The kind priest stopped the film now and then for five minutes to let the images really sink in on the girls watching, and they were so hideous that I, who am pretty tough, had to leave the room before the end because I felt sick and wanted to scream. In an awful state, I went to the youngest nun and asked her why they'd let this filth be shown to us. I told her I didn't like being tricked and obliged to see things I don't want to see – completely false and misleading, disgraceful and disgracing for us democrats and comrades who've carried on the struggle for free abortion on demand. I said that those who made and distributed such 'charming' things should be sued, if only because many of the spectators were girls under 15 who might have been killed by seeing that stuff. The young nun replied that in her opinion the film was 'normal' and that girls with weak hearts (and stomachs) had been asked to leave before the beginning. I should add that these same nuns threw out eight girls, saying they'd tried to abort a friend in their dormitory by giving her a footbath of water, vinegar and salt.

Francesca

Under the dust

Bologna

Freedom! Democracy! Words, words, but what do they mean? I often wonder what so many young women and men partisans died for, when now, in 1977, life is still like it was under the fascist regime, full of continuous fear and uncertainty – not only for political activists, but for ordinary citizens as well. I've never been interested in politics, but now I've got curious and read the papers. It's all an incredible chaos; a city mayor, with all the problems of unemployment, traffic, the university, etc. etc., is worrying about condoms lying around and people sitting on the steps of the cathedral square.

'Bologna, clean city!' That's their slogan. But where is it clean when you need only run your finger over the dust to discover rot underneath? Scandal and corruption everywhere – if we really wanted to do a radical clean up, most of our local politicians would be swept away!

61

Instead they moan about the teenagers, whose only fault is not agreeing with the traditional parties, because they've realised that even the parties which claim to be on the side of the worker and under-dog grasp every opportunity to harm and exclude them even further. They talk about the drug problem and unemployment, but what do they actually do? Nothing! They condemn and exclude these young people as human trash. While those who do something for them, as far as they can, are other young people who are then slandered as subversives and a danger to society.

Excuse me for letting off steam but I feel sick when I hear people talking about psychology and other such nonsense, full of false paternalism.

Diana

Isabella

A month after the death of Isabella Pelloni, comrade in the movement at the faculty of literature and philosophy, Rome, we want to remind the comrades and everyone who knew and loved her of this death.

A month has passed. A month has passed since Isabella decided to give up the struggles, the smiles, the friends won by her gaiety. A month has passed since Isabella turned on the gas, since she 'looked away'. A month has passed: gestures, looks, feelings, speak louder than words. To suddenly realise that someone doesn't exist any more, can't express herself any more, is the greatest, deepest, most terrible pain.

All of the 'unsaid' between ourselves and Isabella is a wound, a space filled with pain.

But this isn't all: it would be human but perhaps selfish. It's she who couldn't go on, who couldn't exist any more . . . our pain is only one side of her choice, everything is mixed in – fear, love, sadness, anger and respect.

It's true, looking to Isabella we will try with all our strength from now on to challenge all our possible choices, our relationships, our tasks.

Isabella has been gone from us for a month.

Paolo, Guidarello, Ettore, Sandra

Against death

Ancona

'As a small child, then they taught you with a whip how to pretend to count, you already thought of death, but no-one knew.'
Jacques Prévert.

In the paper, after the murder of Francesco Lorusso, we published two juxtaposed photographs, both showing an armed soldier at a street corner with a poster behind him. The first was subtitled 'Santiago, September 1973 – armed with helmet and machine gun, hangman Pinochet's man stands in front of a Popular Unity poster of children playing: "The happiness of Chile begins with its kids."' The second was titled 'Bologna, March 1977' and showed one of Kossiga's men, with helmet and tear gas gun about to fire, in front of an LC poster: 'Francesco Lorusso, 25-year-old communist murdered by Andreotti's carabinieri' with the image of an ordinary young militant, one communist among many, *alive*. I'm not sure it was politically correct to link the two photos, but that's not what I'm most concerned about.

There's another, deeper thing, which gets me inside. It's that tearing contrast, the weight that the soldier carries, *the life and death* for all the little children with their flowers, the kite, the ball, the doll, the Unidad Popular flag, and Francesco, shouting out his youth . . .

The two posters, the two executioners.

I'm back in the school where I teach, a secondary school. Seventeen desks in a circle, 17 lives each 13 years long, together we read in the papers about Francesco's life and his death, we even cried in class with great respect for one another.

Staffolo, a village of sharecroppers and bricklayers, gradually leaving for elsewhere. Two thousand people when they're all there.

The children, 13-year-olds. Games, a 'happy' life, *'la felicidad . . . los niños'*. They say they're growing up faster, the young women start menstruating earlier. Laughter, ring o'roses, play, discovery, arguments and quarrels . . . this is supposed to be happiness, the banal best years of your life, and though you say cynically you don't believe it, in your heart of hearts you think so too.

63

At the end of last summer, elsewhere, some 'young' comrades attempted suicide, others got drunk in various ways, lucidly and deliberately. Many of them had a heavy sense of death, brought on by politics, daily life, their needs and frustrations, government propaganda and the bourgeois chants of death, impotence and anger . . . everything together. The sense of death plus making rebellion into a crime: that's what the regime is trying to impose. And heroin: how many young people look death in the face? Self-destruction, as they say.

But it isn't only main-lining, it isn't just for 'youth'. They inject this thing into your head today right from a baby. As a child you haven't even the rights of a black, they decide everything for you and treat you as a puppet – your dad, your family, your school. But it's more than that, it's the unmistakeable sense of death this society gives off so that the daily call to death is present here, in class 2B at Staffolo. For a 13-year-old the photos of Chile and Bologna are proof of the crime, proof that the bosses kill.

In the secondary school at Staffolo they know we are being killed out in the streets and inside, inside our daily lives.

Maurizio (14, repeating a year):
Death comes black, hidden / falls on everyone. / Young and old, / it comes with its scythe / black and hidden.

Lamberta (13):
Someone calls me, / I can't hear / I don't want to hear. / The joy of living / gone. / I'm alone in a house that's too big. / I'm alone. / Alone. Alone.

Patrizia (13):
Woman why do you despair? / Is it because your daughter has died / in a stupid road accident? / Or because your boss / has sacked you / because his factory is losing money? / Or because your son / in a youth demonstration / has been badly wounded? / Perhaps because your husband / has been arrested / drunk and disorderly? / Or because in this world / there's no hope for a better future? / Why? /

64

Roberta and Roberta (both 13):

Cigarette in hand / books and a little room. / All that's left to you. / It's been two years since you laughed. / You hate life, / society. / You'd like to leave this world / but you can't find the courage. / You still hope for a better world, / you've studied for 14 years / what have you learned? / You know how to read and write / but that's all. / Haven't you understood, too? / Yet you go on living in this filthy world, / running away is useless, / you'd never make it.

Luciano (14):

How ugly life is / today you live / tomorrow you die. / A few people mind / everyday about the dead. / I think yesterday's life was good / and today's is agonising. / In the world there are / millions and millions / of people dying / of hunger and leprosy / or seriously ill. / And people / who commit suicide / because of family situations / because of bad luck / out of desperation. / In our village / G. Luconi committed suicide / because of his family situation.

Maurizio (14, failed his last exams):

Peace, peace, children / friends, not hatred / soldiers but friends / soldier friends always / soldiers throw away your guns and take up flowers / don't fight, war is ugly. / Let the dove fly / don't shoot it down, don't let / the cruel eagle kill her / fight, don't let / them kill the dove. / Let her fly. / Why must we die, / it's not right to die killing another / fight not to die. / The soldier about to die asks 'why? why?' / Maybe he leaves a wife and children. / Why, why / we won't die, we'll live. / We'll live / the dream of living to die old / the dream of not dying of war. / Why, why?

Marco (13):

Protest, young student, anyway I'm not listening. / Young student / you go around the streets with banners / saying 'Kossiga we want your head' / but anyway I send my pig-police against you / anyway they'll kill you sooner or later. / Occupy the universities young student / destroy them / anyway I'll build them again with your parents' money. / Young student, destroy the streets of your

65

town, / anyway I'll send my armoured cars in to exterminate you. / Yes, attack me with whatever you like, / kill me, / but I'll go on protesting for my rights.

Calabria, in the 'toe' of Italy, is the poorest region in the country.

The right-wing Catholic organisation Comunione e Liberazione (Communion and Liberation, CL) was instituted round 1974 to contest the political leadership of the marxist left in the schools and universities. In the 1979 university elections, the CL lists came out top in many cities including Milan.

The end of the road

'Outsider', a little while ago this word had a strange flavour for me! Then I was living in Calabria, and pronouncing this word or perhaps introducing it into a discussion was a satisfaction, it tasted almost sweet.

But one fine day, as inevitably happens to many southerners – nobody knows why, or whose fault it is – I found myself, suitcase and railway ticket in hand, bound for Rome!

'I'm going to live in Rome', I said. Yes, I'm leaving for Rome, at last I'm leaving this hole of a village, this shitty environment, these shitty comrades behind me and I'm going to Rome!

There I'll find 'real' comrades, lots of comrades, all of them ready to help me, to give me a hand. They'll accept me, I'll have no problems adapting etc. etc. They'll all be fond of me, they'll discuss things with me even though I'm a southerner, even though they notice my southern accent. They're real comrades, they believe in 'real' justice, real equality etc. etc.

'Outsider', how strange, a word pronounced in two different moments, taking on two different flavours. Now for me, like for so many other southerners, it has a bitter taste.

I came to Rome and the only people who took any interest in me were from CL – refectories closed, the university closed, so no place to meet, no chance to make friends.

The people from CL befriended me. They said 'Come with us
66

even if you don't agree, come and meet Jesus, we'll give you "disinterested" friendship.'

I went.

There I found, I'm sorry to say, lots and lots of southerners, not because they're fascists, not because they're CL, but because they're 'southerners'. They'd given them food and lodging at modest prices, and 'friendship'. After two or three days I left. I'd understood the trick, the mechanism they used to recruit. I'd had enough.

Comrades, I ask you to think about this, about our position as outsiders, about how, when it doesn't lead to a nervous breakdown or suicide, it leads to a CL group.

A southerner

Three youths

Milan

What follows is a letter written by a comrade about a tank crashing into a Fiat 127. The car was carrying three young people who were all killed. The writer is a cousin of one of them.

On Monday night, three young people were massacred on the via Cassia, outside Rome, by a tank which went out of control during a manouevre, crashing into the car they were travelling in.

The report in the press was given two or three lines, as a sort of curiosity.

Nobody pointed out that it isn't normal for three young people going home after a pleasant evening to be crushed by a tank; nobody pointed out that these exercises are done without any precautions either for the soldiers or others, or that every year a lot of young men die or are injured in military service.

They try to pass off these things as accidents, fate, coincidence.

They're making an enquiry into the incident; as usual the conscript driving the tank will be found responsible, instead of the state structure and, specifically, the military machine organised to protect bourgeois power, with its bastard orders, its lack of respect for life, its behaviour modelled on a state at war.

67

My anger stems from the powerlessness I feel in front of this enemy, writing these lines. Anger at the death of Carlino with his love of life, his cheerfulness, his intelligence, his gayness, his goodness killed 'by accident' on Monday night.

Gabriella

Bologna saw its democratic reputation compromised at international level in the months following the March 1977 events, as Judge Catalanotti, a PCI sympathiser, continued to order arrests with the political support of the Communist administration and Mayor Zangheri.

Dear Bruno

Bologna

Dear comrades,
I'm Bruno Giorgini's mother, and I beg you to publish this letter as it's the only way I can tell Bruno how I feel as his mother and comrade, about his disappearance to avoid arrest. [It should be made clear that Bruno has *not* joined the terrorists.]

Dear Bruno, writing to you is very difficult. There are so many reasons why it's difficult that I don't know if you'll understand in the end what I'm trying to say.

First of all I want to say I'm fairly well, so don't worry about me. I hope I'll gradually get back to normal both physically and psychologically.

The anger which tortures me is political anger and a sense of guilt, guilt for not having understood, after 20 years as a communist activist, that we'd end up like this.

When I was very young, together with other comrades in the Resistance, I believed I was fighting for a free world, not only for myself but for the thousands of young people of the next generation; this came up often in the discussions among resistance fighters, many of whom died for that ideal of freedom.

I don't know if you, 'comrade' Zangheri still remember this; I think not, considering how you present yourself whenever you can on television and in the press as the 'Boss of Bologna', with your personal bodyguard, and how you persecute all those who don't knuckle under to the policy of austerity. Thousands of young people are in jail, others, like my son, are underground just because they want work and a better life. In your political obtuseness you don't even realise you've got the wrong target. It's me you should be persecuting because I brought up my children to struggle for a better world; and don't come to me and talk about unity with the Christian Democrats. We want unity with workers, not the employers.

As you see, dear Bruno, I've digressed, but I want you and all persecuted youth to know I'm with you, that I love you all, that I have faith that despite this dark period you'll win through, that the young people who have been killed in the streets with the tacit agreement of the PCI will be avenged.

Please excuse me Bruno, but I can't write any more, I'm crying with anger and pain, I only hope I'll see you again soon.

Your mother,

Adria Giorgini Minghelli

This letter refers to a revolt which started in poverty-stricken Reggio Calabria in the summer of 1970, following the news that the city would not be named capital of the newly instituted region, hence there would not be the hoped-for new jobs. The Communist Party disapproved of the spontaneous rebellion, and its leadership was left to the neo-fascists. On the left, only Lotta Continua sympathised with the revolt, and was accused of being itself fascist. The rebellion flared up sporadically for several months, ending with the military occupation of the city. As a result, the fascists gained electoral ground in the south. Two years later, in 1972, the trade unions finally launched the slogan 'North-south, united in the struggle' and organised a demonstration in Reggio Calabria with the participation of 100,000 workers from the north. The government promised large industrial investments in the area, which were never made.

Calabria, the '70s

Calabria, the '70s. Complete desolation. No work for anyone.

Workers, shopkeepers, professional people struggle on wearily, it's an effort to live. For the young, a future with no prospects. Dockers spend their days on the station steps hoping someone will call them for a job. The old man who sells sweets in front of the cinema complains that he's a communist, yet his son, in order to get to play billiards, hangs around with fascists.

The peasants protest carrying spades and shovels. The women are all united with the consciousness of being citizens. The system has to react firmly. The southerners mustn't start giving trouble now the northern industrialists have so many problems with those bloody unions. But in the '70s a revolutionary moment can't be suffocated by brute force.

What better way to put out a red fire than with a black fascist blanket? And the regime uses every means at its disposal: the press, television, meetings. The number of infiltrators from all over Italy is high, and their task is made easier by men's anger. In two days the miracle is completed: at Reggio Calabria there's a fascist revolt against the institutions . . . organised thugs smash the place up and the system has won. This country may have missed a chance.

Ado

At the end of the following letter the writer lists some of the most notorious political and social scandals of the past decade in Italy. The 1969 piazza Fontana bombs which killed 16 people in Milan were placed by neo-fascists, in connivance with the Italian secret services; in 1976 at Seveso near Milan a cloud of poison gas escaped from a factory contaminating a large area; the Italian rate of fatal accidents at work ('white deaths') is the highest in the EEC; Salmonellosis (food poisoning), like the cholera outbreak in Naples in 1975, is typical of bad hygienic conditions; in 1975 a woman patient in a mental institution died in a fire because she was strapped to a bed. The Communist policy of 'non-opposition' to the Christian-Democrat government ('since Berlinguer decided to give a helping hand', as the writer puts it) did not bring about any notable reforms.

70

I got a shock

Dear comrades,

I'm 34 years old and come from a working-class family, communist from way back. My father was unemployed until he was 35 (1947), first because he was an anti-fascist, then because he was in the PCI (from 1943) and above all because he was a passionate activist, honest and undiplomatic (because even then there was a difference between party bureaucrats and activists and between activist and activist). Right from the moment I was born, you might say I've lived and breathed communism: at home (where my parents read aloud from novels like Gorky's *The Mother*), in the streets and in the doorways of the houses in the working-class district where I lived, then going with my mother to distribute party propaganda and collect signatures against NATO, in the occupied factories where I went with my parents, taking food to the comrades on strike, at the street meetings held by [PCI leaders] Togliatti, Pajetta, Amendola, etc. (who'd still remember them today?)

I read Marx in my adolescence (I remember reading my first lines of Marx with great excitement at 15, during Religious Knowledge), Lenin, Gramsci etc. I can say without exaggeration that social commitment, the struggle against the abuses of power, the struggle for communism, the dream of communism, the obstinate search for communism as the air which would let me breathe, has been the most important fact of my life; communism has been and is the constant poetry of my life, and therefore life itself. When I was 20 I joined the PCI.

Seeing the politics of the PCI from up close, meeting 'communists' who were more representative of the average than my parents, was literally a shock.

To tell the truth, I began to have doubts.

I tried to examine the party's line more carefully, and the doubts certainly didn't go away. But I never had the courage to really go into it. I was always very active, and this saved me from 'thinking' too much. But when the struggle against disgusting manoeuvering and the arrogance of power had to be turned against the PCI itself – now completely identified, at local and national level, with the worst forms of traditional power – I had

71

another, healthy shock. I stopped for a moment and examined everything as scientifically as possible. The result was a conscious, well-thought-out and definitive written resignation in June 1976. My father resigned too at the end of the year.

Now I no longer belong to any party, but I follow your paper with interest. You seem to me to be the only people who, amid obvious but inevitable difficulties, are making a serious political attempt on the left of the PCI, without falling into the trap of trying to rebuild a classic, traditional mini-party under the vast shadow of the PCI. Nor have you withdrawn to an aristocratic position of detached criticism, afraid to dirty your hands with a movement which, besides obviously doing some things right, often makes mistakes as well. I like you because you don't shake with fear every time something seriously wrong happens inside or outside the movement, you don't try to keep a 'respectable' image for the benefit of the people who in reality have provoked the very disorder they rant and rave about. You're the only ones who, whilst rightly dissociating yourselves from the 'armed struggle', have the courage to confront this objectively very difficult and dangerous question without allowing yourselves to be influenced by the hue and cry of those who maintain that the problem of the 'armed struggle' can be solved by immediately dissociating oneself from this or that group, or by enacting increasingly fascist laws, by inciting the workers against all perpetrators of 'acts of violence' and not against the instigators of the piazza Fontana bombs, or those responsible for the Seveso disaster, for the fatal accidents at work, for the deaths of children through salmonella poisoning, for 'crazy' people burnt alive in asylums, for kids who live surrounded by rats, for thirty years of corruption, theft, tax evasion and exploitation, for unemployment, for social injustice which is all getting worse since Berlinguer decided to give a helping hand.

This is the real violence and the principal cause of disorder. It's against this that the unions should firmly mobilise the movement of the employed and unemployed.

Communist greetings,

Luciana Morelli

Radio Alice was a Bologna free radio station opened in 1976 by a group of self-proclaimed 'mao-dadaists'. During the street fighting on 12 March 1977, Radio Alice contributed a running commentary and reported on police movements for the participants; a few hours later the station was raided and all its staff arrested, although the political philosophy of the radio station (named after Alice in Wonderland) was non-violent.

Antonio Mariano was well-known for having played Chopin on a piano dragged out of a café on the 'night of the barricades'.

Antonio Mariano – pianist of the movement

Bologna-

To talk about a friend who isn't with us any more, to say how you feel when you still can't believe what's happened, is the most painful and oppressive thing there is.

To talk about Antonio Mariano, whom a lot of people in Bologna knew, because he studied medicine here for years and had been arrested for participating in Radio Alice, to talk about him today, now we know he'll never be amongst us again, is a terrible thing, words aren't enough.

The usual ordinary, stupid fatal accident has taken him from us.

In the last few months, while my sons have been in prison, he acted towards us like a true comrade, bringing us his exuberant affection, his hope, his participation in our work.

I can't say anything more, I haven't got the strength – I hope others will do it in my place – the memory of his smile will always be with me.

Elena Minnella

His best piece was 'Chicago'

Bologna

I'm a comrade from Bologna, a friend of Antonio's. Now Antonio isn't here any more, he's dead. I could stop here, but I'll go on

73

because it seems to me really absurd that the death of a comrade should be relegated to five lines in *Lotta Continua*.

The life of a comrade is too important, life is always too important, to be liquidated in a few lines. I knew Antonio, though I half don't like saying it because too often when a comrade dies everyone immediately knew him or her.

The same thing happened when Francesco died. Everyone immediately found they knew Francesco; perhaps I saw him at some demonstration, I don't remember, but I felt bad when he died. I knew Antonio though, I've known him for five years. I remember the day I met him, a winter's day in the Margherita park, he was playing the guitar, I went there and we sang and talked and went to piazza Maggiore together.

Other things – suppers at his house, the big meals with lots of people, playing the guitar in piazza Maggiore, 'Antonio, shall we sing something by Crosby, Stills and Nash?' His best song was 'Chicago', I often sang it with him. And then in March, his arrest at the radio station, postcards to the prison: 'We're waiting for you', 'Come out soon'. Then two months later they let him out, but he still felt he was inside, he felt guilty about the comrades still inside while he was free. Every time we met he'd ask me if I'd had any news about the comrades from the radio: Valerio, Mauro, Gabriele.

Then the accident. A stupid death. But perhaps there's no such thing as an intelligent death. Overtaking a coach, an accident.

Antonio has gone. Telephone calls here and there, to the radio. A train to Termoli at night, a seven hour journey, nobody talking, everybody talking, saying that Antonio can't be dead. Then the arrival in a little village, the notices, 'Antonio Mariano, 26 years old, medical student, killed in a road accident.'

Radio Alice tapes of 'Chicago' and Chopin played on the night of the barricades, 12 March.

Antonio wasn't only that, he was more. Francesco is alive and fighting at our side, and Antonio is alive and fighting at our side.

Daniela

74

Feminist Orthodoxy

Milan

Dear sisters,
We want to write you our impressions of the conference on abortion, sexuality etc. held in Milan on 25-26 June.

We want to talk particularly about the general session: there was a 'political' (in the sense of being detached from the personal) debate, speeches which repeated well-known positions just for the sake of repeating them, which were not based on personal experience and appeared to consider women a 'terrain for political agitation or masses for manoeuvre'. Orthodoxy and conformism ruled . . .

We feel this attitude was provoked by the obstinate refusal to talk about ourselves as whole beings. Very little was said about our sexuality with men, which is, after all, what abortions come out of; there was silence about our dependence, submission, love and ties with men; our involvement/love for their power and sexuality.

The material basis of our desires was never mentioned – the appeal of men was taken as a purely ideological fact. We believe it's positive and liberating to go with a man because you like him, because you want pleasure, not security nor his power.

Talk about men seemed to be outside Feminist Orthodoxy, a sign of incomplete liberation, and thus something to hide. In fact, as is often the case, talk of men was noticeably absent from this conference.

We don't know if it's ever happened to you sisters, but in these women's conferences we feel cut off from your desires, interests and curiosity, and feel our curiosity and desires about you are being rejected.

Neither of us have ever felt this sensation in any other meeting of human beings . . . it's evident that we don't love ourselves nor each other, that this engagement with men determines our lives. So why not talk about it? Since we repress any feelings of sexual tension and curiosity there may be between us, on these occasions, all we are left with are power relations. These favour the women who speak well, who are known and who 'speak for' the various collectives. The rest of us are outsiders, who can only follow the leaders.

We wanted to say – but there it would have been a provocation – that we like making love with men, that it's something which involves us, something that we wouldn't dream of giving up, something we'll always do.

We want to develop and realise our desires, we want to make love with human beings – not men or women. We don't want to be obliged yet again to censor/repress our desires and thoughts amongst women, we want to talk together about this male ideology which we share, trying not to be slaves to it, but without hiding it.

It seems to us that for many women the definition of 'feminist' represents another form of false consciousness which prevents us recognising each other, from moving outwards and experimenting.

We also want to add a few words on why we're writing to *Lotta Continua* and *Il Quotidiano dei Lavoratori*: 1) we know it's a contradiction writing these things for papers which are not produced and read by women only; 2) however, we want to communicate these things and we have no other means; 3) we want to communicate with women who are outside any kind of feminist elite and power group – women like us; 4) we think it's time to stop accepting the elitist behaviour that is common in the movement.

Much love,

Valeria and Anna, from the feminist collective 'Le Erinni'

The writer of this letter is Sante Notarnicola's wife. (See notes on pages 42 and 54.)

Notarnicola

Bologna

Dear comrades,

I am writing to tell you that Sante Notarnicola has been transferred to Asinara. The families of the NAP comrades have already written to you about the conditions in which comrades live in that penitentiary. Here I want to tell you how the transfer took place. On Saturday 3 July I saw the comrade in Fossano prison [near Turin] and left at 4 o'clock. When I returned at 6 o'clock with a food parcel as usual, I was told that Sante had been sent to Asinara.

After I had protested 'energetically' the governor of Fossano agreed to see me and when I accused him of having behaved in an infamous way, worthy of the fascist regime, he replied that he hadn't informed me or the comrade of the imminent transfer to avoid a possible 'violent' reaction on the comrade's part.

So this is how they apply those articles of the prison reform bill that state that a prisoner may immediately inform his family of any change in where he is held!

Yesterday I telephoned Asinara penitentiary and spoke to the governor there . . . who knowing me as a left militant, amused himself by saying 'I'm not sure that you're really Notarnicola's wife so I won't tell you if he's here or not.' His evident satisfaction betrayed the fact that the comrade had already arrived (this has been confirmed since from other sources) but I've had no news from Sante himself and, knowing the comrade, I'm sure this isn't due to his laziness.

. . . This lack of news about comrades is common to all the relatives of the comrades at Asinara. Meetings are practically impossible because of the limitations imposed, and anyway are finally at the complete discretion of the governor.

I'll write to you again later and in more detail about the attempts to destroy the communist militants physically and psychologically by concentrating them in special prisons, of which Asinara is only the first in a series, and by keeping them in total isolation, both from the other 'common' prisoners and from each other.

Communist greetings,

S. Berselli Notarnicola

Pissed off

Pescara

What was the good of Rimini, and of what happened after Rimini, if the comrades are still using physical violence?

This happened at Pescara: in the office of Lotta Continua, comrade Alessandro Azzolla beat up a woman comrade, imposing his supremacy as a 'virile' male through violence.

This is confirmation for those who still don't believe that it isn't only the fascists who beat people up.

Alessandro is a comrade who thinks he is good at community work, when he hasn't understood a thing about what the revolution is and how to go about furthering it, or what inter-personal relationships should be like amongst men and women comrades and proletarians. This sort of violence is the weapon of people who feel weak and are on the defensive.

'Your violence is merely impotence.'

Anna Maria

Dear Antonio

Ciao, I'm the girlfriend of Antonio Mariano, the comrade who died in an accident on 30 June, to whom you dedicated the last article in *Lotta Continua* today. I'd like you to publish this letter which perhaps not everyone will understand, that some will see as sickly and heavy, but for me is vitally important because perhaps it's the only way I have of talking with him, of him, for him. Thanks, and lots of love.

It's one of those evenings when I find myself alone with myself, my mind ready to reconsider and analyse everything, strangely lucid. It's nice to sit here writing to you, as I always did up to 15 days ago. I really don't know what to say, as I realise I'm on the verge of tears . . . you know love, this evening too my hands are frozen and I try to find your warm body between the soft sheets of my bed. Hey! Where have you got to? Up to a few moments ago I heard your words, I felt you shivering with cold, I listened, my ear on your stomach, for the gurgles of hunger, I kissed your fresh, sweet lips. But where are you? Oh but where are you? If I could only write words of love to the splendour of your hair, if I could only colour in your heart with the dust of butterfly wings, if I could only caress your lashes with a rainbow, if only you were here, now, like in all our secret moments. Oh love, how these two years have flown by, our first meeting at the station at Termoli, the long afternoons at the house by the sea, those sweet moments of music

78

in the country at Carlo's place, the hurried goodbyes, the kisses, the anxiety, me and you being happy, the letters, the photos, the presents, our home-made jumpers, getting stoned, the rows at home and all . . . all the rest . . . not to mention zapping around on the bike, that old, clanking but oh so sweet bike. There, I knew it, I can't write any more, wait while I get the guitar and I'll make you a present of a song, any song. 'Chicago'. I love you infinitely.

Lilia

Shitting in the countryside

Santa Teresa di Gallura (Sardinia)

Dear comrades,
We're the ones who were driven out of the Valley of the Moon, after an incredible series of provocations.

But let's take it in order: we got here about a week ago, but there were already other people in the caves in the valley. About two days later, going back to the valley through the village about 8 in the evening, we were making a bit of a row (but nothing illegal for that time of day) so a few of the village inhabitants (three) provoked a sort of fight which was sorted out straight away as the great majority of the villagers, though emotionally involved, were not hostile towards us. From that moment a tense atmosphere developed, blown up by the local press, the mayor and two or three neo-fascists, proprietors of the big hotels, who saw their dream of classy tourism collapsing with the arrival of the 'freaks'. Some evenings later there was another provocation when a banger was thrown into the middle of a group of us who were standing in the road. The mayor and council then decided to send a telegram to the Ministry of Internal Affairs, saying they could not cope with an eventual uprising of the local people against the freaks, and therefore requested police reinforcements.

The forces of law and order, about thirty armed police, arrived yesterday morning, occupied the valley and, using absurd and incredible pretexts, ordered us out. The main argument as to why we should go was an 'ecological' one, given the 'extreme danger of shitting in the countryside'. In an atmosphere of this

79

sort, as you can well understand, very serious provocation can occur. A peaceful attitude on our part appeared opportune – but it hasn't helped and it won't last for ever.

In June 1977 three members of an Armed Proletarian Nuclei (NAP) terrorist group were identified in a Rome square. Antonio Lo Muscio was killed in an exchange of gunfire with the police. Maria Pia Vianale and Franca Salerno (who was six months pregnant) were beaten up in public by policemen before being taken away. A photograph of Maria Pia, battered but defiantly raising a clenched fist, was widely publicised and touched off a debate on violence in the feminist movement.

There is a popular feminist slogan 'No more whores, no more madonnas, finally just women'.

The male enemy

Pomezia

I'd like to criticise the communication from the feminists of via Pompeo Magno. The feminist comrades may well react to this criticism from a male by saying 'What the hell does he want, how can he understand "our" problems?' (It's been said to me only too often.) But I'm still writing because, besides being a man, I'm a comrade fighting for the abolition of bourgeois-imposed roles, both masculine and feminine. Now, from the feminists' communication it seems that feminism has nothing to do with class struggle at all, in fact women 'mustn't misplace their anger in a struggle that is not ours', in other words it would have been better, according to them, if Maria Pia had been writing documents in via Pompeo Magno at the time. And they go as far as to say that the form of action chosen by Maria Pia and the other NAP women doesn't flow from *their own* choice, but from a sort of conditioning or psychological dependence on 'male values'. What makes me angriest is that they talk about the 'male enemy' – an abstract male, when our real need is to combat a *sexist* mentality, *those who create it* and *those who take advantage of it,* because let's remember that the 'male' is nothing but a product of bourgeois capitalist society, a role forced on us from above, which we must refuse in the same way we refuse the feminine roles of madonna or whore.

In their communication, the armed struggle is moreover considered, not as an act of revolt against the system (with all the necessary reservations of course) and against the state, but as a 'product of male barbarity'. Hey!! Have we gone crazy?

Sure that I'll be getting some curses from the feminists (though I'd prefer a reply), I salute you with a clenched fist.

Fox

Sisters in jail

Bologna

This letter is to denounce the extremely tense situation existing in the women's section of the San Giovanni in Monte prison, Bologna.

On the afternoon of 28 June, after a quarrel between two prisoners, a head nun called in more than a dozen (male) guards who beat up two women (bruises and abrasions are visible), who had protested against being locked up in their cells before the normal time. Following a report to the administration by the nuns and guards, one of these women was then transferred to a worse prison, at Modena.

And this is just the latest of a series of incidents here, which cannot be officially reported because the women concerned (minors, drug addicts, etc.) are 'unreliable' (their words).

The women who arrive in this prison are treated like whores by the nuns, when they're lucky. We're not allowed in the corridors in low-necked sweaters; they only listen to us when we swear; we have to go to the showers fully clothed, and have to queue up because we're not allowed to go in more than one at a time. The nuns handle all our accounts and expenses without telling us anything; the drug addicts are treated like dirt and left on their own during withdrawal crises.

Any exercise of power over women is rape, and here power is expressed by imposing 'predictable behaviour', taking away every illusion of independent thought. Things are arranged so that we're

81

set one against the other, and our tensions come out in violent and spiteful behaviour amongst ourselves.

But these squalid characters whose job it is to make us believe that the walls surrounding us are very solid, sooner or later will have to think again.

The women prisoners of San Giovanni in Monte

One more case of abuse of power

Dear sisters,

I am writing to report an abuse of power, the last in a long line of such abuses continually imposed on women by our society, by obtuse sexist ideology, by repression and by violence, evidence of fascism today as in the past.

I haven't been raped, no, I underwent his amorous experiments unwittingly, then I became conscious and rebelled. I told him how I felt. And he, Marco di Palma, PCI sympathiser – not even an activist – pretended to understand. Suddenly a quarrel broke out, one of many, sparked by the rage he'd been accumulating for days because of my continued refusals when we were trying to make love. For me, love means gentleness, poetry, harmony between two people who fuse into one. For him . . . maybe the same, in theory. So a fight started and he grabbed me and threw me out, onto the landing. I followed him into the street trying to recreate some sort of dialogue. He tried to drag me home, he slapped me, smiling, getting mad, he twisted my arm and yelled insults at me. Finally two boys intervened.

And then my father, saying I must never raise my head because Marco's a man with his god damned spermatozoa, so he has every right to cancel my last shred of dignity, beat me up and humiliate me – because I'm a woman. This is crazy, sisters, this is real pyschological and physical tyranny over women which is considered normal.

Perhaps this is just an ordinary story, but in a few days I'll be put into someone else's custody – my father wants to give up his paternal rights over me, since he lost face with the neighbours when I screamed my desperation about a boy I thought was different from the other repressed and repressing males. My father

82

doesn't want me any more because I was 'crazy' to scream when I'd been hit. You'll agree, sisters, that to beat up and humiliate a woman is still frighteningly normal. Why should I be put in custody, what crime have I committed?

Sisters, brothers, help me. Make my last desperate appeal for freedom, my appeal against physical and moral violence on women effective. For having rebelled against the slavery of the role imposed on me I risk ending up goodness knows where. Please publish this letter so that people realize that even a little abuse of power will not be tolerated.

With a clenched fist,

Brunella Bernardini

A nuisance to society

Rome

With deep anger and shame, screaming with the pain of my powerlessness, I report a woman's death. I too am an accomplice and murderer, so are all of you, so is everyone. Her name was Ileana, she was twenty-four.

On 14 July she was discharged from the neurological department of the Gemelli hospital and deposited, against her will, in an institution run by nuns (who didn't want her). Discharged from Gemelli as 'cured' (of what illness?) and in excellent physical condition and therefore ready to find a job (!!!) and face life. Alone. After having lived in institutions and mental homes all her life. Excluded, insecure, afraid, desperate. Abandoned, in a hostile environment, outside the 'protection' of the mental home. This was her entry into society. It was her breath of fresh air, her great adventure. On 20 July she committed suicide. She left this poem:

> 'O God
> I've killed myself
> but I already know
> that you've forgiven me.
> The rock of death
> I drew near to
> now I know it was you.'

Ileana, you didn't commit suicide. The violence of our institutions killed you. Together with our indifference, our ignorance, our fear, our inability to communicate with you, our selfishness. The fear of facing a difficult subject, a threat to our stability, to our psychic integrity, the fear of getting involved and so many other things.

I know that Ileana isn't the only one. But how many more like her must die before we become conscious of this reality? This unknown reality of the most excluded women, the ones cancelled from the list of people who have a right to live. Ileana is dead and society is relieved.

I too felt a sense of liberation when she died. Freedom from a responsibility I didn't want. Sisters, who weren't there when I tried to contact you, sisters, who didn't want to listen when I tried to talk about her, this was a woman like us. Let's try to face this problem of women who are alone, forced into mental homes, forced to turn crazily in circles. Until the moment of self-destruction. Can't we fight for them too?

Nucci

See note on p.24.

Our need to live will bury them

Brescia

Dear *LC*,
We're a group of soldier comrades. We're writing to tell you we're having a good time in military service. No, we haven't gone crazy, the truth is that being together here we make the dormitories the centre of a permanent party where we play music, sing, talk about what we want, dance – we've rediscovered a bit of life, and we're *taking it back*, inventing new forms of struggle inside the barracks.

In the last three weeks, we've been having more fun than for a long time past. We've discovered it makes us feel good and makes our superiors feel like death.

Lots of things have happened lately, good and bad, but all very important, with some great discussions in which we've talked about everything from leave to 'restructuring' the army, from the

84

terrible repression we're living under to the anger we want to burst out with, from the punishments they give us to the punishments we give them, etc.

We've realised that our dancing, our songs, what we shout, make them feel really bad, it's made them crack up. The colonel doesn't know what to do any more. The first few days he tried punishment, confinement to barracks, then punishment duty, and today he's threatening us with military prison.

It's great and we're realising that hanging out together, making a row, music, dancing, etc. helps us to understand – that it's our need to live which will bury them.

A clenched fist
from a group of comrades on holiday at the Ottaviani barracks,
Brescia.

PS. To all barracks of the north, centre and south – the Night is ours, let no-one lay a finger on it.

From Giuseppina's mother

Pisa

To all the men and women comrades of Lotta Continua. An endless
emptiness . . . a terrible pain, a torch in my heart.

I am Giuseppina Poggi's mother. I happened to read a cutting from *LC* in which the memory and death of my poor little girl were commemorated with deeply felt words, and I thank you for it.

I still think about your words and cry. I cry because I'm moved, because I feel you with me; I cry out of regret and anger and desperation! I cry not only for the life she had a right to, for those eyes, that hair, for her sweet little hands, for the clenched fist that was so strong, for everything she was and I can never see or touch again . . . But I also cry for what she had in mind, for what she could have done and given.

So little, so steadfast, so strong in her desire to banish injustice from the world. So young, and already so tried, with such a longing to live, to build something together with her Sebastiano, another dear and steadfast comrade.

85

In your words I feel your sadness joined with mine, I feel your torment and burning desire to go on, to take up the tasks and sentiments of my daughter – often contradictory because of her instinctive desire to make choices, to improve . . .

Always on the side of the oppressed, the people who are shoved aside by those determined to get ahead in this world without thinking that beside them are others who suffer, who are weak, excluded, betrayed, who thirst for life and justice in the truest and right sense of the word. I don't know where I've found the strength and pleasure to write to you, while my soul is in turmoil, but I feel I must do it because it brings me together with all of you who have understood and loved my child. Three months after losing her, I want to remind you all of her.

With affection,

Giuseppina's mother

About a suicide

Villafranca

On 25 July 1977, at Cremona, a conscripted airman, Andreino Brocca, committed suicide. He was convalescing at home after having cut his veins in the barracks. The papers talked about rows with a sergeant (!?) and in the barracks they're saying, 'He was crazy. He went home nearly every week. He was very highly strung.' Nobody asks why it happened, or perhaps they don't want to know. Saying this sort of thing is easy and it helps you not to think.

I believe that it was military service that killed him, his being taken away from his world to 'make a man of him'. A man, yes, but only according to their values, functional to a bourgeois, inhumane society which remembers you only to make you produce and suck your blood, or train you to defend the bosses' interests.

I don't want to make a martyr of this man, but at least I'd like to draw an example of what the system is capable of doing to you, simply in order to keep even the smallest cog in place in its filthy social machine.

A fellow conscript

86

Family life

Motta Camastra (Messina)

Dear sisters,
I am a 16-year-old girl, an LC sympathiser. I have been a feminist for about three years, which could be considered heroic, considering the area I live in. Anyway, I'm not writing to you to give you an autobiography, but to send you a cutting from our local paper, the *Gazetta del Sud,* which is the most widely read paper in the province of Messina as well as the most fascist.

The excerpt comments on a tragedy which happened in Messina a couple of days ago: a man threw his wife and two children from the balcony and then went after them. In his will he said he wanted a family grave in order to reaffirm the family unity lost because his wife insisted on her rights, and, as the paper says 'believed that she could claim a share of authority in the management of family affairs', while he wanted a traditional, patriarchal family.

The paper continues with a series of remarks which show how women are seen in Sicily in the year 2,000 (they say we're living in the year 2,000 and this is a civilised society). Well, I don't think I've discovered anything new, every day similar things happen, perhaps less tragic, but still examples of the way a rebellious woman is punished. These events are always aggravated by newspaper comments implying that 'she had it coming to her'. But silence makes me feel like an accomplice – and reading our paper lately, I've realised you feel the same – it's as though I said 'Well, really she *was* asking for it.' Sisters, we've already done a lot, but faced with this sort of thing I think we all realise that an enormous amount remains to be done. We must fight on fearlessly.

Feminist love,

Maria Catena

See note on page 10.
The use of 'collective, horizontal' violence and 'self-managed mass violence' mentioned towards the end of this letter was theorised

by *Autonomia Operaia*, as opposed to the traditional 'elitist' use of violence by the Red Brigades (BR). The theoretician Toni Negri has written: 'The differences between the theories of Autonomia and the ideology of the BR are radical. The BR have an ultra-centralised idea of the party as the fundamental and exclusive arm in the struggle against the state. This is classical Third-Internationalist ideology. Autonomia considers organisation as mass organisation which filters and interprets in reversed form the capitalistic organisation of social production.' And: 'Every act of struggle must be directed to freeing the fundamental needs of the proletariat . . . whereas for the BR, any effort or struggle in this direction is impossible unless the structure of state power has already been destroyed.'

Since June 1979 Negri has been in prison – charged with being a leader of the Red Brigades. The Italian state clearly does not accept that there can be different types of violence.

False heroines

We want to comment on violence (proletarian, male or feminist).

We don't wish to judge in any way the women comrades in the NAP, who have all our solidarity as sisters and victims of state violence. We only want to point out how the active presence of women inside the NAP has brought out many of our contradictions, and has also fired the imaginations of a lot of our male comrades. This goes for the 'Three comrades of Rome' who, with the habitual arrogance of know-alls wrote in *Lotta Continua* (13 July) a heated reply to the letter from the two women's collectives in Rome.

These male comrades have built up their own image of NAP women – heroic, courageous, and completely consistent comrades who have none of the contradictions and weaknesses of the feminists. In reality, the men comrades would like us all to be like that – strong and fearless at their side!

We don't understand why the problem of violence opens up so many contradictions for us, while for them (the men) it isn't a problem at all. For them the only problem about violence is when and how to use it, they don't even try to understand what it is and what it means, because by now they have internalised it to such an extent that it has become part of them. In fact, violence is

88

experienced by them not as a male instrument, but as something innate and natural in the male, the premise that legitimises power and the instrument which reproduces it. Violence is nothing more than power itself, affirmed as such and transmitting its moral values through repressive acts. Thus the idea of violence is instilled in the male (of all social classes) so that he too, to an extent decided by the system, may be a symbol of power.

Violence (that is, the exercise of power) towards women; competitiveness, hierarchy, all this is violence, it is power reproducing itself, forcing those it oppresses and exploits to adopt its ideology, thereby creating stratifications, hierarchies and abuses within what should be class unity.

And so even class struggle is seen as a sort of contest between the armies – those who have power and those who (without questioning it) want to get power. We reject the logic of the army, of obedience and command. We can't imitate our enemies. We can't continue to maintain their mentality and arrogance if we really want to destroy it. And the practice of violence, even when imposed on us, even if only in self-defence, will bring us necessarily to reproduce and accept its mechanism.

That's why we are afraid of violence, because we have always been its victims, because we are familiar with the mechanisms of abuse and exclusion, we know all their implications and consequences. We don't believe that when used by the movement, violence becomes a neutral weapon, like science – today in the hands of the exploiters, tomorrow in the hands of the oppressed. We think it is still something which is completely identified with the idea of male-power-domination-personal-affirmation. We think that violence as such is continually practised by comrades, from the little boy with his toy gun to the 'comrade' who feels he has a perfect right to rape or beat up a woman comrade.

But we don't believe in non-violence, and we don't see it as the only way of struggle for women. Such a powerful enemy can't be defeated without fighting it on its own ground.

But to win we must oppose the enemy with a collective, horizontal violence, not an army of specialists, reproducing violence as hierarchy and discipline within its own ranks.

The choice of the armed NAP and BR groups carries this price, a price which organised women refuse to pay, and which the whole movement must refuse. We don't want to see more of those professionials of 'proletarian violence', demo stewards lined up in military order, jealous of their power, high priests of the karate gymnasiums. We are not rejecting militant self-defence or direct action in pursuit of our objectives; in fact we claim them as rights for everyone, hence also for women. But it's no good talking to us about self-managed mass violence, if we then come up against the usual mechanisms of power and oppression.

We ourselves see, every day, with every act of violence perpetrated against us, how difficult it is for us to react. However, we believe that it is possible to go through a gradual, collective process of rejection-reappropriation to discover our own dimension of violence, which will be at the same time a liberation of our repressed energies for self-defence and a rebellion against the violence that we will otherwise continue to submit to.

Simonetta, Paola, Luisa, Leda, Tiziana, Marina

Women and women

Sciacca (Sicily)

We read the article [from Catanzaro] in *LC* no. 175, an article which claimed to represent the condition of women in the south.

In fact this article reflected the backwardness and cultural tradition from which these girls cannot (or don't want to) liberate themselves. It is simply absurd to extend the sometimes disconcerting implications of this article to all southern women.

We live in a small Sicilian town, and our environment is much the same as (probably worse than) that of the girls from Cantanzaro . . . nevertheless we reject the idea of delegation evident in this article. We reject particularly any reformist solutions to the problem of family and couple relationships.

We are firmly convinced that seeing the institution of the family and 'exclusive' relationships as a source of security and support, or not having the courage to oppose a mistaken marriage because of a sense of insecurity, represent 'blasphemies' unworthy of a group who call themselves feminist. This is a moment of crisis in the feminist movement and we can't now try for a new sort of 'couple relationship'. We must above all go for independence, independence from the family, from 'him' – and not try to justify or reform rotten institutions like the family or submit to sexist relationships because of the old need for protection.

We therefore ask these pseudo-feminists not to think their point of view applies to all southern girls, and to begin to really think in a different way, freeing themselves from a series of problems like the need for 'security' and 'protection', which must really cease to exist for the militant feminist movement.

Pina and Margherita

Women in the south

Caltagirone (Sicily)

Dear sisters,
Is the Garden of Eden at Sciacca? We are comrades and – perhaps – feminists, from Caltagirone, so we're from the south too. Maybe we haven't managed to free ourselves from our cultural backwardness, but a lot of us in our town think that the remarks made by the women comrades of Catanzaro are not absurd and shocking, but analyses of real contradictions which many women, even feminists, experience. With this, we don't presume to reflect the conditions of all women living in the south, as judging from the tone of your letter, you appear to do.

In particular we don't accept your way of presenting yourselves as the true feminists handing out instructions to the whole movement.

It's right, dear sisters, that 'we must above all go for independence', but it's also true that up to now we've lived with our families, that we've received a particular sort of up-bringing and a particular set of values, that we live in a male-dominated society, made to measure for men, and there's no space for the woman who wants to affirm herself as a woman-person.

These ties and these values are not easy to shake off . . .

I (O.C.) am one of the many southern comrades who couldn't take it any more and six months ago I left 'in search of independence'. But it hasn't been easy.

Looking for a job I experienced sex-discrimination (even for work without cards), I experienced my own weaknesses as a woman which I hadn't felt before. Although previously I was in constant conflict with my family and with other people, and was independent of any relationship with a man, I've discovered that in fact my family provided a sense of security for me, a security which I then sought (and luckily didn't find) in the couple relationship. Now I'm slowly trying to find that security in myself, but it's a long struggle.

By describing what has happened to one of us, we wanted to say that the elements of weakness and insecurity pointed out by the women of Catanzaro are real, because we are a product of bourgeois education aimed at making us fragile and insecure – people with something missing. Once we are aware that our weakness is a 'social' and not a 'natural' fact, we can recognise our need to affirm ourselves as we are, and not as they want us to be. The weakness is inside us and we, at least, come up against it every day.

We think our struggle for independence is not isolated, but touches on all aspects of this society. From the struggle against capital for guaranteed work for women, which is the first step in our emancipation, to the struggle against bourgeois ideology, or rather its organs of transmission: the family, people, men, including comrades, who are often very clever at adapting our issues for their own use.

Communist and feminist greetings,

Some southern women comrades

Perhaps this letter will be of no use

Perugia

Perhaps this letter will be no use. I've always been surrounded by trouble and I think I always will be. About two months ago in a nearby town a feminist committed suicide by throwing herself off the bridge, and on the rocks below she found her new freedom.

Her relations, friends and acquaintances hushed up this

event by admitting she was a drug addict and hadn't known how to accept the life of 'Jesus our saviour'!

Yes, that same life that pushed her to suicide. For me, who knew her, it was a different story. I met her on a demonstration at Perugia, and after talking about how disgusting Italy was, she told me she was gay. That's right, 'one of those', as we 'comrades' call them. At first they seem to us 'different', 'abnormal'.

We condemn them, we kill them with a torture which isn't what the nazis used (or is it?) but something worse – exclusion. She told me she couldn't go on for much longer with this life. She kept her promise, and now her desire to love has been 'smashed' on the rocks, there under the bridge.

But I'm forgetting, we're civilised, so we can't understand those who refuse our civilisation, who want to invent a new kind of love. If I try to talk about my homosexuality to friends (who call themselves 'comrades'), they start laughing and using that ironical, witty back-chat – positively conventional by now. These are the anti-conformists! the defiant extra-parliamentarians!

As a gay person I accept myself as I am, even if I find barriers everywhere, in every conversation. But even though I accept myself and my own personality, I'll come to the same end as all the others – drugs and violent death. What fine speeches get made on violence and repression! But don't you understand that what you are doing to me and to all gays is violence and repression?

Perhaps this letter will be of no use, because by the time you read it I'll be with Anna in our new freedom! Or perhaps there's someone who wants to help me!?? No, that's impossible, you're civilised and couldn't stoop so low! Anyway I enclose 1000 lire for your paper. But I ask a favour: let's start to talk about being gay because there have already been too many victims. We've had enough!

With a clenched fist,

A gay man

PS. If anyone agrees with me let's get in contact and begin the struggle against bourgeois civilisation, which imposes certain norms on our sexuality as well.

'The pain of those blows'

Rome

Dear comrades,

Near Rome there's a beach where you can sunbathe nude undisturbed apart from occasional forays by the forces of law and order. Many of us gays often meet up there and find ourselves caught in the ferocious and disgusting crossfire between the 'respectable bourgeois families' and the diligent intervention of the forces of law and order.

For a brief moment we had the illusion that the ghettoes in which we're confined were a little wider than the ideology of normality would admit.

Event: three of us were walking naked along the seashore, 100 metres outside the limits of the nudist area. Result: 30 people assaulted us, first with the usual words (that really is a classless vocabulary!), then physically. As often happens, the lynchers of the gays were working class or petty bourgeois, and in this case they weren't only men, since their 'women' encouraged them like in some medieval joust.

Comrades, until the pain of those blows wears off don't talk to us any more about workers-struggling-for-the-revolution, nor about feminism. Later, calmly, we can reason things out.

With confirmed queerness

As arrest warrants continued to be issued in Bologna following the March events, a group of French and Italian intellectuals accused the Communist administration of deliberately repressing the opposition. Mayor Zangheri invited them to come and see for themselves that 'Bologna was the freest city in Europe'. The writer of this letter sarcastically quotes the subsequent Communist Party assertion that 'Italy was the freest country in the world.' In the name of the movement, the intellectuals then convened a 'Conference on Repression' in Bologna for September. (See page 110.)

94

One big hug of solidarity

Rome

Comrades,

I am the mother of Vittoria Papale, political prisoner – alleged NAP member arrested in her own home – who has been waiting trial for one year and who must therefore be presumed innocent.

Morally and physically raped, in contempt of every human right laid down by the constitution, held without any evidence against her, just because she knew Tuzzolino – engaged to her foreman's niece – when this man was not yet connected with the anti-terrorist police force but worked with horses.

After her arrest she was placed in solitary confinement at Rebibbia (Rome), then sent to the penitentiary (sic!) at Trani, then back again for a few days to Rebibbia, then on to Florence prison and then to Pisa. Requests to the Ministry of Justice that she be transferred nearer to Rome (her little boy suffers from asthma and cannot travel very far) were refused, as was her right to be in close contact with her lawyers and her family. I can only say . . . that this is the truth about what happens under our 'government of law' in the 'freest country in the world'. I ask you to publish the thoughts I include here. It will be a way of showing my daughter I'm with her, and with all political prisoners, subjected to injustice and violence.

Thank you,

Evy Papale

To my girl, who has as a cell-companion her communist faith:

The repressive state has managed to shut in your bodies / but the roofs and walls of the vile prisons / which drip water, hatred and injustice / will never destroy your ideals / those ideals which with moral and physical violence / they try in vain to extinguish in your hearts / and which free in your minds / beyond the bars / reach the comrades and become a shout / a shout in their need for a human dimension / a shout which will unify and involve us all / a shout of faith and freedom and love / which no repression / will ever kill / because to the voices of the prisoners and the free / the

95

exploited and the excluded / will be joined the voice of the murdered workers / calling for justice and revenge.

Your mother

Let the people serve themselves

With great disappointment and incredulity I'm writing to you about the article which appeared in our paper *Lotta Continua,* which up to now I believed to be, if not the most, at least one of the more serious and honest papers. I'm talking about the centre pages – 'October Jubilee – a real task', where the USSR was presented in bucolic tones as a country where, yes, some things are wrong, but all things considered is a pretty good place. I could write a whole article refuting word for word what the comrade from Bologna wrote, but for the moment I'll just ask him which Russians he has talked to. Because, first of all, Russians are not the Soviet Union; or have we forgotten that Russia borders on the west with West Germany, Austria, Yugoslavia, etc., and on the east with China? And that from Europe to the Bering Straits these busy Russian comrades have 'converted to communism' a lot of different peoples – what does someone from Mongolia have in common with a Russian from Leningrad? Or Breznev's dictatorship which is interfering in China too?

Why do I care if the young Russians know western pop music and are pacifists, when Soviet foreign policy competes with the USA in colonising every possible part of the world. Ask the Hungarian, Czech, Rumanian and Polish comrades whether the Soviets are so generous and nice! Certainly if I go to Moscow and talk to a political leader's son and go and see him in his home, there's no difference between him and me. But let's not only go to Moscow, let's talk with the ordinary people and try asking them about politics. I personally have often tried to talk politics in these so-called communist countries – their usual reaction has been fear, ignorance, or a couldn't care less attitude. How many convinced communists are there in the USSR? And does the mafia exist only in Sicily?

We must completely support the Chinese exposure of the USSR, a state whose one objective is to sovietise the whole of Europe.

96

What I've never understood is that sense of shame or loyalty which makes so many comrades try to defend or at least minimise the very serious things happening here on the left, and defend at all costs the actions of states which call themselves communist, but which unfortunately are something quite different. A passport is a right which cannot be denied, and no argument will ever convince me that a state which builds walls and triple fortifications with police dogs and turrets on their borders, where they shoot first and ask questions later and where the real comrades are sent to asylums, is a good state.

Well, comrades, I totally support the struggle against the Asinara system [high security prison for political prisoners], but I can also assure you that wherever there is an Asinara (and unfortunately the Asinaras are not only in Chile, Argentina, etc.) no-one will ever convince me that it's for the good of the people, or the state, or communism. And Stalin's crimes, even if they were perpetrated in good faith, for the good of the people, were still crimes. I know this can be seen as sentimentality but for me communism also means liberation, and I completely agree with Mauro Spadaro's point in his letter published Saturday 13 September, that when we carry on a vast campaign against food additives in Italy, for example E123, and point out the rotten exploitation at the expense of people's lives, or just the lack of hygiene, we should also go and look at the toilets, shops and restaurants of the countries of the eastern bloc. Let's go to Rumania for example and complain about the long list of noxious food wrappings, or go to the Soviet Union to hold a peace march, from Leningrad to the Ussuri for example, or, why not, in Red Square to demonstrate against nuclear power stations . . .

Livio S.

PS. We've had enough of those who serve the people, wouldn't it be better for the people to serve themselves as they want to, or aren't they mature enough?

The writer discusses an incident which took place during the festival of the opposition press held in Milan in July 1977, when activists of the MLS attacked participants mistaken for members of Autonomia with heavy frying pans. The MLS, a neo-Stalinist group with little influence outside Milan, had long been known for its military style and use of physical violence (spanners and iron bars) against political opponents and rivals.

Opposition to whom?

Cuneo

Dear comrades,
I am a comrade detained in the 'model' prison at Cuneo; before my arrest I was working for Falck in the 'Vittorio' factory at Sesto San Giovanni, now I'm in a prison workshop making social outcasts. I'm one of the seven workers arrested at Verbania on 22 April this year for 'carrying arms' –needless to say we're the victims of so big a frame-up that the state can hardly handle it. While we were in prison serving our two-year sentence, a further warrant for arrest for 'subversive association and membership of armed groups' was issued, relating to an episode of workers' mobilisation at Magneti Marelli during which the files that management had on the workers disappeared, and were 'found again' later in a Red Brigades base.

I want to say something about what happened at Ravizza park in Milan during the Festival of the opposition press. From the account of the meeting I read in *Lotta Continua,* more time and energy was spent in opposition between left groups than in opposing the class enemy.

Will the left never be able to work together? Also with rank and file comrades of the PCI or at least all those who consider themselves anti-capitalist, without resorting to beating each other with frying-pans etc.?

Now, everyone engaged in class struggle risks the cruellest posible accusation – being made to appear a criminal. So many comrades found themselves inside the state prisons, and they have put up with . . . not frying-pans' blows, but everything a hunter can do to his animal prey after he's captured it! And these comrades inside have to go on reading in the so-called revolutionary press about the stupidest thing comrades can do – beat up other comrades!

What are these acts supposed to demonstrate? That you're the 'best'? That you've understood the 'right line' to bring about communism? One thing's for sure. Until we reach that objective – communism – no-one can say 'my strategy is the winning one'! Obviously I'm not going to say which is the winning 'strategic line', not out of opportunism, but out of consistency!

I too have been a member of the PCI and I left because they wouldn't explain what the extra-parliamentary opposition was about!

And until I've reached the objective I've set myself – i.e. communism – I'll never be able to say that the 'right line' is this or that!

Everybody knows, though, that the only alternative is revolution – and because capitalism wants it that way, we'll have to use any means we think suitable. We'll have to use those same weapons that capitalism has invented to defend its supremacy.

I therefore appeal to all those who consider themselves anti-capitalist and who are involved in class struggle: put your energies into studying every tactic and if one of you doesn't agree with another, don't resort to certain methods and don't go and denounce that comrade to the police or anyone else, as seems to have been happening!

As I've already said – I don't want to be moralistic or paternalistic – I'm just a comrade who suffered a lot reading articles like that one and who, like all of us, has a heart – a revolutionary heart, but also a human heart! I don't want us to go on fighting each other. I think that every comrade, what-ever his 'political line', most dearly wants the class struggle to go on everywhere, in the factories, schools, neighbourhoods, etc.

I very much hope that there will be answers to my letter – negative or positive, I don't mind. My heart has been freed of a great weight . . . even though at times I cry, it's certainly not out of weakness, but out of love for all comrades. The class struggle needs every bit of energy. One day, maybe, we can all meet around one fireplace and tell stories about how this or that comrade used a frying-pan on another – to let off steam, unless we hear of a better reason.

One thing also to the feminist comrades: we respect every principle of struggle that you think it best to adopt. Already women are subjected to male violence . . . Who are we to judge the choice made by comrades Maria Pia, Franca, Mara or those who, like them, may have decided to pick up the gun?

Isn't the physical and moral suffering they're going through enough, without adding the violence of those who call themselves their sisters? Who negate through their criticism the choice made by these women?

The carabinieri report on me, made in the course of enquiries, was 'he's violent'. On the contrary, I consider myself 'a violated person, born a proletarian, a communist from the beginning'.

I repeat: I'll accept any criticism, but I don't want unreasoned attacks. I've written this letter not to criticise but to understand! For now I'll content myself with 'words'. Afterwards I'll do a deeper analysis. And if anyone can give me further enlightenment I'll be grateful.

Communist greetings,

Riccardo Paris

Is there a communist way of loving?

This letter has perhaps been inspired by the desire to understand a bit more about what relationships between comrades are, how we experience them and whether 'by chance' communism has anything to do with it.

All our relationships are based on a series of reciprocal expectations; we're incapable of loving someone for himself or herself, in his or her totality; we create myths, images, and we love someone for what he or she represents for us, we tend to make that person the centre of our world, and we want to be the centre for him or her. We see love as necessarily linked to sacrifice and pain, to self-renunciation, but also to possessiveness, jealousy, fear, power and therefore selfishness. We tend to create a scale of feelings, sentiments, emotions: for a friend we feel affection, for our 'favourites' love, for flowers liking. There's a whole graded list which has to be respected, the system we live in has invaded our deepest feelings, it uses a false conception of love to destroy us all, men and women alike. They call all this love, but it's just a negation of the meaning of real liberty, simplicity and respect for ourselves and others. The rejection of all this, and learning to recognise our own conditioning, our own limits, our conflicts – self-examination, self-acceptance, and after that a spontaneous change within ourselves, could mean a communist way of loving.

In reality, a one-to-one relationship is often a safety-valve for our frustrations (as activists, or from our difficult childhood, our dad, our mum, our grandparents, etc.). You get hold of someone and give him or her a dramatic account of your problems, you whine a bit on his or her shoulder, and the relationship seems complete. This is just exploiting someone and then maybe being exploited in turn.

Then there are the 'beautiful' relationships (the ones you talk about to make yourself feel good): when you're with a girl or boy who seems to give you everything and you say you're giving everything too. Then all those fine speeches (the 'open' couple, growing together, etc.) are forgotten. You build yourselves a private island and forbid anyone to set foot on it. You're together every day, then every hour, always more! And in the end when he or she looks at someone else, it means that he or she hasn't understood a bloody thing, is a 'prick' or a 'cow' etc. The one who feels betrayed 'suffers from jealousy' (but didn't we tell each other that jealousy means lack of trust?) then the crisis blows up, the quarrels, everything confirms that when a certain level has been reached in a relationship (in this case, the 'object' to go hand in hand to all the demonstrations) then you're no longer interested in moving forward, but just in keeping possession of what has been won.

This is how the best 'comrades' turn into the worst 'bourgeois'.

A lot of these comrades claim to be 'anti-romantic', 'real revolutionaries' against bourgeois frivolity (personally speaking, if romantic means flowers and the moon – we are romantics!)

We believe that being communist means at least setting oneself the problem of living one's life as a totality. And we don't believe that 'since society is bourgeois, only when we have

101

communism – paradise on earth? – will we be able to change personal relationships', but that the two things are closely connected and must advance together.

Struggle, the building of communism, is also a different way of living and being together. We must have the courage to question all our attitudes, so that a relationship doesn't mean giving what we want to give and taking what we need – but accepting and offering.

Daniela and Gioacchino

PS. We believe that the revolutionary press gives too little space to these problems, so this (very confused) letter was written by both of us so that there'd already be a discussion in it.

Homosexuality and revolution

Turin

I'm a Turinese girl and I'd like to reply to the comrade from Perugia who wrote a rightly angry letter about the death of that lesbian; rightly angry, but still too weak and resigned, considering what the movement for sexual liberation has achieved over the past five years and is still achieving. I'm from Fuori! Donna ['Come Out! Women', the Radical Party organisation] but Fuori! isn't the only gay movement in existence. There are COM (Milan), COSR (Revolutionary Left Collective), COP and others. You ask for help saying you could end up as the lesbian comrade did, but you say nothing at all about your, our, movement. You look for understanding from the comrades, but you aspire to suicide; though you can identify with a certain sort of struggle, you still feel the weight of sexism which a lot of comrades still haven't questioned.

But our struggle, the gay struggle, isn't separation or ghettoisation. It's a struggle which takes as its starting point the 'gayness' of the rediscovery of our sexuality, of our way of being, of having acquired, after 2,000 years of fear and guilt, the confidence which makes us shout in the streets 'Gay is beautiful' and not only 'queer or lesbian is beautiful', transforming a language that has always been used as pornography. It's a struggle

102

which will put suicide off for a good while, because together – but only together – we've been able to do it; at least we've made a few people think, and scandalised and horrified others, and that is very important.

Ciao to everyone,

Rossana Pittatore of Fuori! Donna

Who reads that stuff?

Motta Camastra (Messina)

Dear comrades,

Here I am, I'm a 16-year-old woman comrade writing to tell you about the repression I've been undergoing these last few days from my 'parents'. The problem began when (1 June) *LC* arrived at the newsagents in my village (I personally requested it). And obviously in a village – 1,000 inhabitants – of conventional people, fascists and reactionaries, that makes news and everyone starts asking 'Who is reading that stuff?'

My parents even blackmailed me, 'If you don't do as we say, we'll stop that paper' (sic). Then, since looking for another comrade here is like looking for gold in a rubbish dump and I had (and have) a big need to discuss things, I decided to get in contact with comrades through the paper, by letter. At the beginning everything went smoothly, my parents agreed to hand over letters addressed to me unopened. However, in the last few days this 'pact' has gone to pot. They read my letters, and my mother told me 'I don't like *Lotta Continua* and if you go on reading it I'll throw you out.' My father had the good (or bad) taste to use different words, but basically said the same thing: 'Listen, I decide what's good for you and what isn't, and if I tell you I don't like Lotta Continua then you mustn't sympathise with this organisation, or I won't pay for you to go to school any more. And these letters have got to stop straight away. You can find friends in the village.' As you can imagine, I felt like smashing everything, especially the faces of . . . well, never mind. What am I going to do? Perhaps from tomorrow I'll be another of those 'runaway girls', certainly I'll continue in my crime of supporting LC and writing to comrades.

103

Anyway, I wanted to tell you this, because even though this repression isn't as violent as Kossiga et al. it's just as significant.

Maria Catena

Why he shaved his head

Montelupo Fiorentino

Dear comrades,
I refer to a letter published by our paper which related briefly how a comrade from Foggia was committed to the criminal asylum of Montelupo Fiorentino.

On this we've obtained some very interesting details: Alfredo was committed to an asylum because, after having been jailed on the charge of insulting a public official, and having waited a whole week for the judge to see him, he decided to protest by shaving his head. For the reactionary judges this was tangible and unequivocal proof that the comrade was mad (like anyone else who rebels or protests). He was immediately transferred to the Montelupo asylum, notorious for the bad way its 'guests' are in (last June a boy of twenty-two committed suicide). The usual practice in these cases is for the patient to be transferred to jail to await trial only after he has been pronounced sane again by a psychiatrist. This means that Alfredo's stay here, which has already lasted more than two months, may be extended for another two months, and that really will threaten his mental stability.

We therefore again ask the lawyer comrades of Tuscany to contact Alfredo and give him at least the legal aid he needs.
Communist greetings,

Pierino
Alfredo Munno
c/o the Criminal Asylum

Feminist, speak to me

Genoa

Dear comrades,
I've been wanting to write this letter for a long time, but I've not
104

had the time, nor, to tell the truth, the courage. The fact is, I've got some terrible problems in relation to the feminists and unfortunately we talk too little about the subject – i.e. the correct attitude to take towards them – probably out of fear. Fear on the one hand of being attacked as 'sexists, chauvinists', and on the other hand (my personal experience) of being dismissed as 'the one who defends those hysterical women, he must be a bit queer'. So I'd like to open up a debate in your/our paper dealing more or less with these points:

1) What's the attitude of the feminists to those men who refuse – as I sincerely try to do – the traditional man/woman relationship and make an effort to overcome all the social conditionings and the sexist mentality which are imposed on us, as well?

2) Is it possible for a man not to be chauvinistic, or even to support the feminist movement, and to be recognised as such by the women comrades?

3) What is the model of behaviour which the feminists think can bring a man towards this ideal? Please believe me, sisters, that an answer to this is vital for me and, I think, other comrades, because I can't and won't believe that a person who calls herself a communist can refuse or, worse, categorise another person as an enemy simply because he is a male, without giving him a chance of showing he's a brother and 'united in the struggle'.

4) Don't these sisters believe that they could and should make more effort to involve the comrades in their particular struggles, helping these men emerge from the above-mentioned conditioning?

There are probably a lot more points for discussion, so I ask all of you – and I think there must be a lot – who feel these problems, to add something. Of course, I'd like a feminist to answer me, if only to insult me – even though I think that wouldn't resolve much, it would be better than ignoring a problem I feel very intensely. Excuse my writing style and incorrect vocabulary, but the thieving system only let me go to school up to the third form and then shoved me into a factory.

Franco, a young worker

In September 1977, when this letter was written, the draft bill legalising abortion in Italy was under discussion in parliament. It was

105

finally passed the following year. Although the text had serious limitations (the main one being that a minor needs her parents' permission to get an abortion) it nevertheless represented one of the most important civil gains of the last thirty years in Italy, achieved thanks to the efforts of the small Radical Party and the women's movement. The CISA, linked to the Radical Party, had been clandestinely organising safe abortions for several years.

Does the women's movement understand women?

When I heard about how the July meeting in Milan of the women's movement, the CISA, and I don't know which other groups (I wasn't there), had decided to stop performing abortions, I was very doubtful about the correctness of the decision, but I didn't have much time to think about it, being in the third month of pregnancy. I went to the CISA, still hopeful that it would help me. There were a hundred women, maybe more, listening to a sister explaining why the decision was taken: 'CISA shouldn't go on providing the solution to a problem which the political parties refuse to resolve, we don't want to be an abortion factory any longer. In Italy abortions aren't being performed any more, those who need one can go to London for £160, everything included.' Right, I thought, right, but not very clear. No to being an abortion factory, yes to exporting abortions – that means going on helping the state out with its 'hot potato', only this time by passing it on to an English clinic, very happy to take our money.

The only difference from before is no-one gets their hands dirty? And the women, those legendary, exploited, raped and conditioned women, what are they supposed to do? (A consciousness-raising group, knitting baby clothes?) Hmm. To go on with the story, they handed out a leaflet which, among other information, stated, '£65 for sterilisation' (for women, obviously). Then they say someone from CISA will go with you, those who are furthest into pregnancy leave first. We give our names and are told little or nothing about what will happen to us.

Is this the politics of self-help clinics? But perhaps the woman comrade who comes with us will have time to explain.

106

Let's hope so. At last we leave, 27 of us. At the air terminal, we're told a CISA woman comrade will meet us in London. We leave, 10 hours late, from Milan airport, but at the English airport there's no CISA comrade. We keep hoping she'll be at the hotel. But she isn't, and after a few hours the younger women get organised, get someone to telephone the clinic. They're not expecting us there. Didn't CISA tell them? By now we've realised the whole thing wasn't organised. Finally, we reach our 'goal', an interpreter 'interrogates' us, then the interview with the doctor: 'Why are you doing it? Does your father know?' (I'm over 18.) 'Why not? Your mother, the boy you go out with . . . ?' While you answer he's giggling with the interpreter. Is this the interview our draft abortion law provides for?

Then the medical visits, the tests. They send us back to the hotel. The morning after, we come back for the 'operation'. You come into the room and don't even have time to undress before you're anaesthetised. You come round after a while feeling bad, not only physically. You're crying, you need someone sympathetic, and the nurses mimic you and laugh in your face. Where's the comrade from CISA? Three of us have an induced birth (8–15 hours of labour). Another six are sterilised, four of them decided on the spot. We couldn't convince them that that wasn't the only way not to have any more babies, any more abortions.

The next day we're taken back to Italy. Four don't come back with us (the three who had an induced birth, and one of the girls who had herself sterilised, on oxygen since the previous night). The five young sisters, comrades, are angry, they want answers to their questions. We ask CISA and the movement: is this the battle for free abortion on demand? Will this happen to women in Italy if the law is passed? And in the meantime will we go on exporting our abortions? Will we still let women have abortions and sterilisation operations without explaining and helping them? Sisters, let's come out of the closed world of our collectives, let's meet other women, start from their real, urgent needs. Let's get it into our heads that the women who 'hold up half the sky' have six children, don't go on demonstrations because their husbands beat them for it, and get themselves sterilised so as not to cause 'problems' for their husbands.

107

It's terrible to suspect that the women's movement doesn't understand women.

Comrades, this isn't meant to be a hysterical, unprincipled attack, it's meant as a deeply felt contribution to a debate in the movement.

A woman

Let us not leave so wide a gap

I'm writing these lines because a comrade of ours has committed suicide. Unfortunately, this sort of thing is becoming more and more frequent; it's not even news any more. But when a boy you've struggled with and enjoyed life with dies, you can't help being shocked and feeling a belated sense of guilt.

It's true, when someone dies like this you can't even shout 'The police are murderers.' We imagined the death of a comrade differently, killed by fascists or by the police, and us out in the streets shouting our anger, demonstrating our grief. Of course Roberto was killed by the enemy, the most evil enemy – our filthy crisis-ridden society. But this answer isn't good enough. To die on the barricades with a red flag in your hand and your girl clasped tightly to you (like in one of those wonderful posters of May '68 in France) would be beautiful, heroic, virile! Some of us in our fantasies have seen ourselves dying trying to stop a tank in a coup d'état or during an assault on our Winter Palace. But to die like that, alone, on an August day, in a car full of exhaust fumes, no! To die like that is inhuman. We have to look each other in the face, ask if we too have killed him, if we too have died a little with him.

Years ago we thought the revolution was waiting just around the corner, courteous and smiling. We were moving fast and firmly towards the 'decisive moment'. But a great many 'decisive moments' passed and everything seemed to be just the same. That little delay, irrelevant on history's calendar, became the measure of a defeat for many. In contrast with this 'exasperating slowness', our lives sped on quickly, taking away our youth, pushing us towards jobs which either weren't there or were drudgery. 'The bourgeois state must be smashed, it can't be changed' we shouted; and now here you are, obliged to live within the same old damned,

108

mocking 'relations of production'. But that's only half the story. If that was all, we could just say our political clock was fast.

The second half of the story could begin by recalling that in 1968 we said that 'everything is political'. This was said in the opposite sense to today's expression 'the personal is political'. It meant that to make the revolution we had to give up our personal needs, hide our emotions . . .

When the hope of a rapid victory faded and political work became hard and uncertain, our 'care-free' social life showed signs of strain. And it was very difficult to 're-convert' our ways of thinking, to rediscover (collectively) our repressed individuality, to find the humility to talk about our personal problems. It was easier to go for private solutions, let ourselves go, break up into little groups, easier to realise we were alone and sometimes desperate. This (luckily) is not the whole story. Feminist comrades have developed the rediscovery of the political through the personal; young comrades avoid the old traps.

This comrade's death was no chance. He died because we have been 'inhuman', all of us, Roberto included, victims of a certain way of being politically active. It was inhuman to send the comrades to the factory gates to fend for themselves, inhuman the way we treated the 'silent' comrades who hardly ever spoke at meetings, or the ones we called 'dummies', because when they spoke they said (badly) things which seemed obvious. The system of big and little leaders, repositories of knowledge and power, was inhuman and so were our relationships at the gates with the workers, seen only as sources of news, as readers of our leaflets, or people to explain the revolution to. How many comrades have we lost on the way – alienated by this way of being political? Who remembers their faces, who ever heard their stories? Who helped them to grow politically, to feel comfortable in our offices?

Roberto is dead and it's stupid and rhetorical to mouth those typical phrases – 'we'll struggle for him too', 'he'll always be at our side', it's cynical to say that perhaps Roberto did not die in vain. It would mean finding a posthumous justification for this horrible death. But amongst the many motives impelling us to change our political and personal behaviour there is also the desire that no comrades should be obliged to leave us like this again; there's the hope that the gap between our splendid theory of the future

109

flowing with milk and honey and our 'squalid' daily practice will never again open wide enough to swallow up the life of a man.

A comrade of Roberto's

In September 1977, the 'Conference on Repression' promoted by a group of French and Italian intellectuals was held in Bologna with the support of all the forces to the left of the Italian Communist Party. Preparation for the conference had taken on the character of a denunciation of PCI repression. The party first opposed the meeting ('a desperate petty-bourgeois insurrectionary attempt'), then decided to accept the challenge and work towards showing that Bologna was an exemplary democratic city. The citizens were invited to be tolerant and debate with the visitors; the local authorities assigned camping space and promised a food supply at political prices. The 100,000 young people arriving with their sleeping bags found the shops and bars open, the populace cordial, the weather sunny. Any violence would have appeared gratuitous, clearly the fault of the demonstrators.

During a ferocious confrontation between the various groups at the Indoor Sports Stadium, the others dissociated themselves from Autonomia, who argued that incidents during the final procession (which had been forbidden to enter piazza Maggiore, the main square) would effectively show up the PCI as a repressive force. By decision of the movement, the final procession through the town on Sunday afternoon, which had been anticipated as likely to turn into a pitched battle with the heavy police contingents, was peaceful and 'creative' in character.

In the autumn the PCI organised a conference in Rome to analyse why the party was so alien to Italian youth.

I talked to Marta at the bar

They've understood nothing about our conference. (How awful to grow old, comrade leaders of the Communist Party!)

I only want to say that these last days I've been happy, that Sunday, the demonstration, the comrades, was the best day of my life, that at the age of 35 I found a new place in the movement. For

110

the first time I wanted/WANTED to be a steward, because it was GOOD to be one, in these days at last I talked with men and women comrades, with my wife, with my son, let no-one dream of isolating the comrades by using me, let no-one dream of imposing his views on me. I talked with Renzo in piazza Maggiore, and listened to him, I talked with Marta at the bar, I'd never have done that before, I hugged Albert (what a hug!) telling each other what we'd experienced for hours, I've got no line in my head, but just the certainty of having moved forward with the comrades, I'm not going to go back again, *Lotta Continua* you're always in my heart, but the movement is my true love.

Franco – an old comrade

A train's going by

Mantua

Dear comrades,
The debate opened up in the paper, to which a great many comrades have contributed with political analyses of the present situation has not, in my opinion, considered another aspect of repression which affects so many, comrades and workers – sexual repression, which includes the difficulty and isolation of any attempt to question the male/female relationship.

What makes me angry is that very often repression in these matters is carried on by comrades inside the movement, showing that they haven't understood they're doing exactly what capital and the revisionists want them to, i.e. prevent us trying to improve relationships and ways of living, by opening up the contradictions and discussing them in order to try and live life, and not give it away to those who exploit us. I'm talking about these things because I'm living out an experience which is making me understand the importance of all this in daily life.

I'm living this experience with a woman comrade whom I've insisted on calling mine for four years, and who is now claiming her independence with all her force, making me realise the shit in which I've been crawling, despite all the fine words and speeches I've always made about autonomy, sexuality and the male/female contradiction. The moment she claimed this desire of hers to live,

111

to have new experiences with other people, and refused the every-dayness of an old, institutionalised relationship which had no more room for imagination and happiness, my security fell apart, leaving me with no protection against a request I had hoped would never come. I'm going through a very bad, tense period, looking for something which will help me get over this experience in a positive way, trying to grow, to question my role as a hypocritical, false, possessive bastard and basically even banal male.

That's why I'm taking every opportunity I can to discuss this, particularly with comrades, male comrades, to try and find a way, a thousand ways, of relating between us men as well. Something more than the pat on the shoulder or political discussion, a way of giving and asking from a comrade that warmth, sincerity and understanding which we all need, especially at this moment.

There are some questions which occur to me spontaneously now and which I don't know how to answer.

Are we, as men, really ready to give up the many privileges we have in relation to women? Do all the things we've said on the question indicate our desire to change, or are we basically trying to get through the tempest with the minimum of damage to ourselves?

Do we or don't we want to change these shitty relationships? I'd have a lot more to say, but it's not possible here.

With a clenched fist,

Giulio

PS. I hope you publish this letter because it's also a way for me to communicate with a male comrade whom I haven't been able to talk to because of the absurd rivalry situation created when we've been together.

To 'create a monster' means to incite public hatred against the alleged author of an odious crime. The first 'monster on the front page' was Pietro Valpreda, the anarchist dancer falsely accused of placing the piazza Fontana bombs in 1969.

Giuliano Naria, a worker

Genoa

More than a year ago a 'monster' appeared on the front pages of the newspapers and on the TV news, and stayed there for a long time – Giuliano Naria, a worker, a comrade, alleged to have participated directly in the killing of Judge Coco and two policemen.

Even before his arrest, he had been blackened in public opinion: described as blood-thirsty, a red (or black) terrorist, a professional killer. The 'lynching' began straight after the event. His photograph in various sizes became familiar, and some (of the many) witnesses felt they recognised him as one of the killers.

Naria was arrested (he had tried to avoid the warrant) with a revolver in his pocket. He was repeatedly confronted with the witnesses, but things weren't going well for the examining judges (the official charge of murder was issued only some time later). No-one knows how many witnesses there were, or how many of these identified him, or how that identification was made (after all the photographs published and the savage campaign against him).

Comrade Naria has always lived in Genoa, and was well known, particularly in that part of the town, because he often went to meetings and demonstrations at the university (a few yards away from the scene of the crime). Now it seems peculiar, positively absurd, that someone so well known in the area should personally participate in an armed terrorist action there.

We suspect that it was a safe, sure solution to pick on Naria, to make a monster of him, considering his background and the present situation.

His family is working class, his father has an industrial disease. Naria himself is a factory worker, sacked for so-called 'absenteeism' and 'lack of discipline', who used to go on extremist demonstrations (more often called in the press 'hooliganism'). In addition, at that time he seemed to have disappeared, so there were all the ingredients for considering him 'different', 'strange', an 'outsider', and therefore capable of killing.

Naria was just a worker who didn't accept exploitation, death at work, destruction of his personality; he was therefore very sensitive to abuses and acted accordingly (without accepting the compromises many of us workers resort to). For this he was

113

sacked, got morally lynched by the bourgeoisie, and was finally labelled a ferocious criminal.

We're not interested in knowing his political and ideological opinions or whether he was in a group or not. We want the evidence for the crime he is alleged to have committed to be made public before the trial. (When will it be held?)

We want the conspiracy of silence surrounding him to be broken, so everyone can hear about his present condition, how he is being treated in one of those special prisons and whether his friends and family can meet him, talk to him and hug him.

We don't have any illusions, we know all about the intrigues of power, but we'd like this case to be re-opened to public opinion, so that when the trial is held the atmosphere is different and in the meantime his conditions in prison can be discussed.

We can say that almost all of the workers who knew Naria are convinced that he had nothing to do with the crime he is accused of.

A group of Ansaldo workers

In October 1977, a student named Walter Rossi was shot dead by fascists in Rome. During the protest demonstration next day in Turin, a well-known fascist hangout called the 'Blue Angel' bar was attacked and set on fire. Roberto Crescenzio, a 19-year-old with no political convictions who happened to be there, was fatally burned. The Turin nucleus of Lotta Continua took the position that Roberto's death, although regrettable, was part of the price that had to be paid for militant anti-fascism. The debate on the subject anticipated the great discussion on the Moro kidnapping six months later, when Lotta Continua *decided on a 'humanitarian' line of defending human life on principle. This position was criticised with contempt by* Autonomia.

What value has a human life?

I'd like to know how far it's right to react to the death of a comrade, I'd like to know how far we can risk other people's lives, without at least considering the problem of the consequences . . .

114

When I heard about Walter Rossi's death on television, I was furious, I wouldn't have given a penny for the life of any fascist. But when I heard that a boy was dying of burns in Turin, I rebelled. 'Bastards, fascists, that's enough', was all I could think. I hated those who attacked that bar more than the fascists.

Just tell me, what difference is there between that boy and Walter? Or does anger cancel the value of life? I can't accept an anger without humanity.

It's a terrible contradiction. Certainly you can't stand around doing nothing when a comrade is killed, but is it right for another boy to be killed? Is it right not to worry about other people's lives?

On the last page of *LC* I read a terrifying report from Rome: 'The fascist headquarters caught fire, there was a loud explosion when a gas cylinder burst, nobody was hurt, the police charged, etc. A young boy passing on a moped was grazed by a bullet . . .'

Everything is on the same level then? The attack on the fascist headquarters, the explosion of the cylinder, the police, and the wounded boy? And what if someone had died in the explosion?

I don't know what the answer is, but I can't take that boy burned in the bar, and I can't bear the fact that for so many comrades he is a sad but inevitable consequence of a correct action.

How right is a struggle which in the name of a new humanity ignores the value of human life?

Donatella

Bifo (Franco Berardi), one of the promoters of the Bologna free radio station Alice, moved to Paris to avoid arrest after the March events. The popular Bifo sent a message written in 'transversal' (mao-dadaist) language to the 'Conference on Repression'.

This language is repressive

Now Bifo is repressing us as well! After the 'Conference on Repression' I thought over my experience during the three days in Bologna.

There is a lot to say, but if I described all my impressions I'd be taking up precious space. What I'm going to say may seem minor compared to all the other experiences of those three days, but for me it's important. As we know, Bifo has gone underground, so it wasn't healthy for him to show himself at Bologna. However, he decided to make his voice heard all the same, through a letter (read by Pino on Friday afternoon at the Indoor Stadium).

Bifo's contribution begins like this (actual words): 'We have to go against the stream even when the stream is going against the stream.' For simplicity's sake, I'll summarise crudely: if the stream (communism) is fighting against the counter-current (capital) we must still go against the stream: no, dear Bifo, I will not go against the stream. I may be a sheep but I'll follow the stream, the undersigned will never stand on the same side as the bosses. I imagine he wanted to say something else as well, I don't doubt it, but for god's sake, comrades, he could have used different language!

I've thought a lot about the meaning of this sentence, but I still haven't understood a thing. Probably I'm a cretin, but there were a lot of us looking at each other in amazement when Pino read those words, so a lot of comrades must be cretins (or not?). This language is repression. Those are condescending words coming from a political star (now international) and they do us violence. I leave these disquisitions to the intellectual drawing rooms; to ordinary people they sound like a piss-take. We don't only need guns in the revolution, we need a way of communicating with the masses, and this requires simplicity and immediacy. If these words had been said at a factory meeting they'd have been howled down (actually, even at the Stadium there was a lot of booing). We all know that the revolution can't be carried out only by the vanguard intellectuals (who understand everything, are good theorisers etc.) – without the working class, failure would be inevitable. There's a lot of work to be done inside the factory, getting rid of the social-democratic logic imposed by the historical left, and I don't think Bifo's sort of language will solve anything.

Perhaps Brecht was right, or rather he certainly was, when he said that simplicity is the most difficult thing; I would add that simplicity is revolutionary. To conclude, I'd like to quote some remarks by Mao on internal democracy in the movement and

116

particularly on who should speak at meetings: 'Communists must listen to the opinions of non-communists, and give them the chance to express themselves. If what they say is correct, they should be applauded and their ideas should be used. If what they say is wrong they must be allowed to express themselves just the same' (21 November 1941). For 'non-communists' read 'those not belonging to your group', because despite everything all the groups still exist.

Ciao and good luck with your work,

Renzo

So now the children are at it too

Avellino

Dear comrades,
Seventy children between the ages of 6 and 12 marched by themselves in a procession through the streets of this city to the town hall to back a demand for public parks. This demonstration, which raised lovely slogans like 'The parks are ours, and we'll take them' and 'Grass, at once and organised', left the good people of Avellino aghast, and also two carabinieri, who on hearing the slogans put their heads in their hands and said 'so now the children are at it too!'

After stopping at the town hall the procession went on down the high street, attracting a lot of people who clapped in solidarity with the children. The demonstration ended up in a district where all the participants agreed to organise properly to obtain for public use a private area of grass which has been fenced in for years.

Avellino comrades

Walter's death and who was behind it

Rome

Dear comrades,
I'm writing this letter about the murder of comrade Rossi, and hope you'll publish it because, after having participated in the

117

recent demonstrations and having felt and breathed the anger of us all, I think it's necessary to remind everyone of something which is certainly not new to the comrades, but which the anger and hatred about what's happened could make us forget. Amid all the questions and doubts in my mind, there's one certainty: fascists, fascism isn't a 'psychological' or ideological movement, but capital's deliberate reply, at an organisational level, to the victories and struggles of its class enemies.

. . . A serious fascist crime turns public attention towards a clearly defined enemy 'external' to the democratic political life of the country, an enemy which isn't capital, but a 'regurgitation from the past' coming from a world defined by frustrations and irrationality; something which has only vague connections with the present via some sections of Christian Democracy, for example. To concentrate on the struggle against the fascists and their cells is, in my view, wrong for two reasons:
1) Because in this way we mask the identity of the enemy and give an alibi to all the political forces which hide behind anti-fascism, taking good care not to take up anti-capitalist positions.
2) Because it betrays the level of demands and consciousness reached by the movement in this last year.

Altogether, comrades, if we are communists and not just anti-fascists, I believe it's because we don't struggle against the hand of capital but against capital itself. It's capital's headquarters that must be blown up, not just those of the fascists, to revenge the death of comrade Rossi.

Fernanda

In an hour Roberto

Turin

Dear comrades,
In an hour Roberto Crescenzio's funeral will take place. During these last few days of meetings and discussions I've been asking myself why on earth all this has happened, why, faced with state repression, and a situation becoming more difficult every day, our active reply, right and necessary as it was, has had such a high price: the death of a boy like us, a victim of this society. Somehow,

118

in a way I can't analyse clearly, in these years we've gone wrong somewhere; a gap has been created between 'old' and 'young' comrades. We haven't been able to keep the debate open, and now I've got the impression that the 'young' and the 'old ' sometimes speak two completely different languages. In order to face the political, economic and social situation, we must heal this split, we must get back together, we must start talking and arguing again.

I don't know how, but together we'll find the way. As long as we're divided in front of an enemy who is strong and united, we'll be nothing but victims, victims like Walter Rossi, like Roberto Crescenzio, like each one of us.

Chiara Colli

Life and its value

Comrades,
Donatella's letter entitled 'What value has a human life?' and yesterday's page on 'We can't delegate anti-fascism' have made me think hard, and I imagine I'm not the only one.

If Donatella's question: 'How right is a struggle which in the name of a new humanity forgets the value of human life?' raised problems for us women, why not get together to work out a way of making our militant anti-fascism a really new form of struggle, no longer sterile and isolated? Why don't we find the way to think about things together, sharing our experiences and maybe proposing our forms of struggle to the movement? After all, as women we know fascism well, considering that it reaches into every corner of our lives right from birth.

This could be the opportunity to give new life to the feminist movement, at a moment when it appears tired and in need of new unifying issues. Through this paper, which all we militant sisters, young and not so young, read with increasing hope, why don't we try to organise a conference which takes up our anger and the conflicts that we experience as committed anti-fascist women?

Marta
119

Reality is different

I'm a 16-year-old comrade and an assiduous reader of the paper, and I wanted to answer Donatella's letter, because I too believe in the value and respect for human life. When the fascists killed comrade Walter I felt really bad, and I was furious too, because I was completely powerless in the face of what happened. But have those people who threw fire bombs and attacked the MSI headquarters really resolved anything? Comrades, for me reality is different, the fascists are afraid, they know we're wiping them out, so faced by danger they react like wolves, killing.

So Cossiga trembles and sends his forces against us, but we are many and determined to fight, and I'm sure we can win even without molotov cocktails and the P38 guns.

Fabio

At Bologna we didn't 'behave nicely'

Livorno

I'd like to say something on the article the Scandicci comrades published on the page of debate about Bologna, 6 October. These comrades seem to have been seduced by the bourgeois and revisionist press; according to them at Bologna the movement lost and 'democracy' won.

This is all false: it's not true that we 'behaved nicely' at Bologna, that there was a noticeable lack of courage and therefore a lack of political will. The movement showed a high level of political maturity; it managed to refuse the military conflict which the state, with the support of the media, was preparing; we managed to win the confidence of the Bolognese working class, showing that we weren't barbarians come to raze the city to the ground, but the real opposition to the regime of the historical compromise. The self-discipline shown by the comrades, the debates between ourselves and rank and file Communist Party comrades in hundreds of small groups, in the streets, opened up contradictions between the rank and file and the leadership in the Bologna PCI, contradictions which the movement in Bologna must learn to exploit if we want to extend the opposition to cover

120

all exploited members of society, and not just leave it in the hands of the 'non-guaranteed'.

To accept a military clash with the state machine would have been suicide – remember there were fifty M113 tanks, units with dogs, bulldozers for breaking down barricades, and 6,000 police. There would have been arrests, and probably comrades killed by the police; to take piazza Maggiore wouldn't have meant much and a big demonstration would have run the risk of disintegrating in the same way as on that horrifying day of 12 March in Rome.

Comrade Clarino

PS. I reject the inhuman and abhorrent thinking of the comrades from Scandicci who end up saying: 'If we had broken the police and military lines, almost certainly a few dozen comrades would be in prison today, but on the other hand this risk is part of our choice as revolutionaries.'

Comrades, we are not machines, nor soldiers in an army of supermen, but communist men and women who believe that it's a political victory when none of us are imprisoned or die in the streets, when *we* impose on the state the level of conflict which suits us.

The need to be happy

Ivrea

Dear comrades,
When I think about Bologna, I remember the happy, moved smile that came over an unknown sister's face when, astride a boy's shoulders, she discovered with amazement how big that extra-ordinary, unforgettable procession was. That procession said, more than anything else could, that the chief thing underlying the meeting at Bologna, in the hearts of thousands of comrades, was the need to be happy. It was this basic 'demand' which brought us there to express a need which is not ours alone, but felt by millions of young and not so young, crushed by this inhuman, crisis-ridden society.

In piazza Maggiore, talking to the city folk, we often told them we'd come because there are no jobs, and everyone sympathised.

121

If we struggle, in reality it's because we want our whole life to change. It's a pity that feelings and thoughts can't take on a physical form – you would have seen people arriving with enormous burdens: hopes, unsatisfied needs, the desire to understand, to know. I don't know if the demand for happiness is marxist, but at Bologna we understood that communism is first of all a rich and contradictory human experience.

During those three days of 'communism on earth' we saw that a lot of problems are still unsolved. We wanted to talk and instead we felt fear in the heavy, aggressive meetings, run by the old and new leadership; we wanted to communicate with each other, and often it was difficult to escape from the confines of the small group; we wanted to understand, and often we couldn't follow the debates; we wanted to be happy and sometimes we felt alone and discouraged. There are still so many obstacles in our way. This dying capitalism is creating a greater and greater suffering for more and more people. Paradoxically, this is our strength, the inevitability of the revolution.

People are beginning to realise that either we must destroy this infernal machine or it will destroy us, it will force us into an existence unworthy of human beings.

We want to learn to speak to the masses about these things: we want to take back words so that collectively we can build a party which doesn't just belong to a chosen few ready to turn their presumed intellectual superiority against us; we want to use our repressed intelligence to develop a theory which will go beyond the sacred and inviolable marxist dogmas.

'Be realistic, ask the impossible', said the comrades of May '68 in France. Right, we want to be happy!

Michele

I'm not going back

Rome

Dear comrades,
Yesterday I went to Walter Rossi's funeral. There were an enormous lot of people there, I saw a lot of comrades crying, and most of them had only heard of him after he was killed.

122

Everytime I heard the slogan 'Walter is alive and struggling with us', I thought, yes, Walter is alive in our minds (but for how long), but now he's cold, still, in a coffin: a 20-year-old boy. Only 20. So much will to struggle, probably so much anger, and so much will to live, like us. And a bullet killed all his hopes, all his fears, all his will to struggle together with us all, to change this rotten country.

I couldn't cry yesterday. I let off steam, later, shouting slogans in via Merulana; furious, like tens of thousands of comrades. Yesterday afternoon I had a new experience: I found myself in the middle of the clashes with the police. I wasn't afraid, because it was no accident, I'd chosen to be there: I wanted to be one of those who were going to destroy the fascist cell on Colle Oppio. So I went up to the front. Then the police suddenly fired tear gas canisters and I fell back a little. Meanwhile the procession had broken up, there weren't many of us left.

At that moment I decided to stay with the others. It was a very lucid decision because I'd already seen the tear gas fly.

That afternoon I saw the canisters whizzing over our heads and falling to the ground, giving out that suffocating smoke which seems to burn your throat, I saw panic on a lot of faces, I felt my skin burning, I saw the deserted streets, like the set for some war film, I saw a frightened man running with a baby in his arms, I saw an old man who had been caught up in all this by chance being comforted by two comrades, I heard of comrades who had been injured by the canisters, I was thrilled when I heard that the fascist cell in piazza Tuscola had been blown up.

Then later at home I felt bad and I'm still very upset. I even want to cry. Every so often one of those scenes comes into my mind, especially the charge in via Merulana; I see the canisters coming continuously, the smoke-filled streets and the comrades sheltering behind cars, the police and carabinieri standing there like cold, evil robots, the broken windows, the comrades' anger, sometimes expressed in the wrong way: what has smashing shop windows and workers' cars to do with the class struggle and anti-fascism?

I can understand violence, if it's against fascist headquarters – I've had stones and cobbles in my hand, but I would never throw them at windows or cars. We need the approval of the people, the

123

people who threw down lemons and potatoes [against the tear gas] from the windows.

Violence must not be irrational.

Violence must be one of the methods used to destroy fascism, not a means of venting our personal anger, which is then turned back onto ourselves.

Yesterday's events have really confused my mind; now I need time to think, to re-examine, to analyse my ideas on how the class struggle should be carried on.

One afternoon, not even a particularly 'hot' one, was enough to make me think, and to confuse the ideas I thought were so clear. I don't want to get caught up and take these things like a game, like a film; if I must use violence against fascism and against the state I want to do it in a rational way, not be dragged into 'guerilla warfare' in the excitement of the moment.

Then this morning, I heard that the boy from the Turin bar had died.

Hell, he hadn't done anything. Whatever the radio and the television may have said, using his death against the movement, the fact remains that that boy died like Walter Rossi died.

And this too makes me think, makes me feel bad. I don't want to fight against people whom I don't consider enemies.

I hope the comrades, willingly or not, will help me to understand.

I only know one thing: what happened yesterday represented an initiation into violent struggle for me. I don't think that next time I'll keep out of it, but as I said, I need to clarify my ideas. I don't believe in blind, exasperated, irrational violence – sought at any cost.

A sister from San Paolo, Rome – one of
many 'stray dogs' with no political home

Two generations

Dear comrades of *Lotta Continua*,
I'm a pensioner from the centre of Genoa. Please convey through your newspaper my heartfelt condolences to the mother of comrade Rossi, killed by the fascist swine.

124

Comrades, I'm tired and disgusted, but I have faith in you young people who are carrying on our struggle. I'm sure that if we are all united, like so many years ago, we'll manage to crush them. As for us old comrades, we'll make an effort to be with you in the front lines, and it must be a great joy to have fighting with you so many comrades who have been in the struggle for over thirty years.

Long live the partisan struggle, death to fascism.

Greetings with a clenched fist from your comrade,

Pina Marozzelli

A necessary crisis

Rome

Dear comrades,

It's been many years since I last wrote. Perhaps this letter can contribute to the debate going on in the movement. It's also a message for certain Rome comrades, with whom I have a few things to clear up.

Cristina, I hope you remember me, I'm the bloke with the moustache you met in Bologna, the one you talked to at length, and intensely, about your problems, your griefs, your joys. I remember you.

It's Sunday and I'm alone. The woman comrade I live with is outside Rome with some other comrades. I didn't want to go with them, maybe because I've understood her need to be alone with other comrades, to be with other people as a woman and not as a couple. It's very difficult to get out of the stereotype mentality of the couple, especially when the other comrades still see you as such. I wouldn't like you to think I've been 'good' to get out of the way and allow her some space: it was she who 'claimed' this space, and helped me understand it calmly.

Perhaps calm is an inadequate word because the road is long, difficult and tiring, and I don't know where it leads. But the view is great. Recently, we've had several rows because of our inability to look within ourselves, but some things have been cleared up, though the price was high. We've understood that we're important to each other, but that the phase of the closed couple has finished for us, that we have unsatisfied needs. When you open your eyes

125

and become conscious, you can't go back, the only choice is to move forward.

It's a big risk, but we must run it. My lover is strong and determined. She doesn't talk a lot, but she moves forward. I'm discovering her in a new dimension. I'm rediscovering myself as well, my desire to live, to love, to get out and struggle in the streets. In Bologna I felt very close to you.

Your world is very different, I realise that, but we're fighting the same battle, you a woman from the south, a wife and a mother; me a petty-bourgeois man angry at the system and himself. When I demonstrated against the death of Walter, for life, I thought about you, geographically distant, but close to me. It's sad that it should be someone dead who shouts for the right to live.

I've got a thousand confused things in my head. I spend my nights talking with comrades, men and women. We're trying to find a different way of being together, we're trying to beat hypocrisy, mistrust, reserve; to start from our limitations in order to overcome them, not to be ideological, to bare ourselves in all our reality. It's difficult. I'm tired, I don't sleep very much, I smoke a lot, but I don't know any other way. I want to try and live out all my feelings, without holding back on anything, with as little ambiguity as possible.

I feel that this personal crisis is necessary, I feel OK at feeling bad, because I've got faith – tomorrow depends on what I am today, on how I can manage this crisis, and on my ability to be alone and accept myself.

Will we meet again in Rome?

Silvio

The newspaper was in the small room

Aula (Massa Carrara)

Because of your newspaper my son has left home. Why *Lotta Continua*? There's been no peace ever since your paper appeared in my home. In *LC* you read only about hatred against someone or other and even against parents.

Now Maurizio has left home: please make him come back

through your paper! He's unwell, he's got a breakdown and I'm afraid.

Tell him to come home, because nobody hates him here. His father hadn't spoken to him for a month because of that business he knows about, but he's miserable.

I don't know if I can bear such a blow. Maurizio suffered because of the rows with his father, and now he's gone. Tell him to come back, please. We don't know where he might be. Tell him that the papers and the books were in the small room, if only he'd asked . . .

Maurizio, please come home! You didn't have to make that big scene at home about a newspaper, or perhaps it was something else. Don't you think about me? Do you think I don't suffer like you over the situation we found ourselves in?

Maurizio's mother

Amanda, 12, an anarchist comrade

Dear comrades,

I'm a 12-year-old anarchist girl. It may seem odd that I already have a political belief at my age, but when they killed comrade Lorusso in Bologna it opened my eyes and I tried to find out as much as I could about the world around me and I understood that the only solution was to reject this state and to build something that will (at last) be just!

Now comrade Walter is dead too and I cried with anger for him and because we're powerless (I and other young people) against this shit state which is busy, between debates, supporting fascist violence and ignoring the bodies of the murdered comrades.

I also want to reply to comrade Ciro (*LC* 9 October) to tell him that probably whoever threw the molotov cocktail into the 'Blue Angel' bar in Turin is sorry for the death of an innocent boy, and my anger at this act is immense, but I myself, after having seen the pool of blood under Walter's body, might have acted in the same way. The armed struggle is an important fact which I think should be used in extreme cases with some understanding of what the consequences of such violent acts may be; I don't approve either, but frankly, after what happened in Rome, I'd have liked to

127

burn down everything. The fascists are bastards and I hate them as much as you do, but we must be careful not to play into their hands.

I'd like some answers.

Please publish my letter.

Greetings with a clenched fist,

Comrade Amanda (A)

Vasectomy – male birth control

Sisters and brothers,

I feel the need to write to give you some information about a male birth control method used by me, but unknown and prohibited in Italy – vasectomy. Let me say straightaway that I had the operation in Switzerland for £100.

I enclose a document with technical explanations about the operation.

The main reason I had the vasectomy (I should mention I have a 21-month-old daughter) is because the capitalist system denies our children the right to grow up in freedom, and oppresses their personalities in order to prepare them for a future as robots; we parents, relations etc. (comrades or not) are their first masters (and this is very serious).

Now I'd like to make some personal observations:

1) The pill, like any chemical product, is harmful for our bodies (in this case the woman pays).

2) If vasectomy is forbidden and unknown in Italy it's up to the movement to publicise it and find ways to make it possible to have this operation in Italy (why only abortion?)

3) What effect will it have on the super-male comrades to know that by altering their own virility they can avoid abortions and unwanted children?

I hope this (very critical) letter will be published and will open up discussion.

With a clenched fist,

Tarik

128

We can meet up

*For comrade Cristiana who wrote in the
paper (14 October) that letter about her
loneliness, the tears she shed 'in silence'.*

Dear Cristiana,
Like you I feel an impotent anger and a need to 'meet' people
stripped of political labels and differences of sex. Not only me but
also Amalia and Franco, the comrades with whom I'm particularly
trying to put this need into practice, and to build up a real feeling.
They often feel lost, lost politically and as people, everywhere.
There are 10 years between us, Cristiana, but I believe age
differences constitute yet another gap between people only in this
system, where the thousands of divisions in work, politics, love,
sex . . . age serve to keep the system going. We feel the same anger
as you, the same anguish, but we also believe that it's possible to
meet the real 'persona' behind the stereotypes which imprison us. I
have experienced it . . . magic moments which it's hard to make
continuous in the brutality of everyday life. None of us, much less
on a collective basis, has been able to make these moments
'permanent'.

I have no method to propose (perhaps we can find it
together) and I have no illusions, we have no illusions, that this will
happen tomorrow. I can tell you, from my own experience, that
the need for a different quality of life must be satisfied through a
collective and then mass acquisition, in order to overturn the old
abuses and injustices, because I myself, in those rare moments,
have found inside myself a unity as woman, communist and
person, a unity which helped me to a better relationship with the
world outside.

We think our need to communicate with you makes sense,
though without any too immediate expectations, and that it could
develop into a real contact.

Anna, Amalia, Franco

In October 1977, three members of the Rote Armee Fraktion (RAF)
129

*held in the high security German prison of Stammheim were found
dead and a fourth seriously wounded. The official version stated that
these were suicides; in Italy it was immediately and widely assumed
that these prisoners had been killed on state orders. The writer of this
letter is an economist who has published a number of essays and
works on computers.*

No sense in the differences

The murder of the German comrades who survived the destruction
of the RAF poses me some moral problems which I fear are far
removed from those which concern most comrades (at least those
who write and have been published on the letters page) on the
question of violence.

I want to begin by saying that however they lived, and
whatever differences separate me from them, these comrades died
as communists. In a moral climate of demobilisation, retreat and
complacency at our own powerlessness, the German comrades
died giving us a lesson of rare idealism and extraordinary courage
– let's try to imagine their last moments when they faced their
assassins – and also indicating a way forward for our struggle. The
enormous political error committed with these murders will soon
become apparent to the social-democratic police. Ulrike, Andreas,
Gudrun and the other murdered comrades – and all the others
who soon will be – can now begin a new revolutionary struggle if
we are all capable of drawing the right lesson from their deaths.

From their deaths, it's exactly that; in this case, too, a
communist must learn to silence his heart and use his brain. 'Take
back our lives' we shout in our demonstrations: this is a sign of the
results of the revolutionary struggle, the crowning of the
communist revolution. But too many people, too often all of us,
forget – it's convenient, very convenient – that 'a communist is a
dead man on holiday', to quote Eugene Levinè, president of the
Bavarian soviet, assassinated in 1919 by the fathers of Strauss,
Schmidt and Hitler. Let's take back death, then, because I'm
afraid that today this is a transitional stage on the road to
revolution. Death and life are not separate like today and
tomorrow, there is no 'Great Wall of China' between them. At
demonstrations, at work, on the street or in the family, in

capitalism they walk side by side. We can forget it, but notoriously the ostrich is not the cleverest of animals. We can say, write and above all believe, that the conquest of life is for now. But then there's Lorusso, there's Walter Rossi, there are the German comrades, there are those who die every day for communism . . .

Whatever the differences and the conflicts we may have had with the RAF comrades, today these differences have no sense, because the lesson their death has given us has overtaken and annulled them: their struggle has become ours. And as for their murderers, we can repeat that history has pilloried them, and the congratulations of all the 'democrats' of all the 'civilised nations' will not be enough to redeem them.

Communist greetings,

Renato Levrero

Lea Melandri is a well-known Milan writer. Like other Italian feminists, she uses categories taken from psychoanalysis, particularly the school of Jacques Lacan.

When death becomes a symbol

I've been very glad to see the 'Little Anthology of Radical Thought' reappear in the paper.

After Mother Jones of the miners and the Sicilian women peasants (an article I really liked), I was afraid we would be flooded with a series of edifying examples, all the more grotesque considering the present less than heroic atmosphere in the women's movement – an atmosphere of hospitals, of medicines, of little reforms, little laws for little neighbourhood clinics, for the great, incurable ills of womankind. I don't like 'nurses', 'first aiders' 'professionals of other people's suffering' and lugubrious discussions on abortion, but I'm equally disturbed, reading *LC*, by the growing anti-fascist sentimentality and rhetoric in the comments which follow the death of a comrade in the streets.

Some years ago, when the streets were filled with red flags, I saw two comrades die at home clutching a common gas tube. Few of us cried then, and each of us knew that they were crying for

131

themselves, for the irreducible substance of our imaginary fears, for all the questions the political struggle left unresolved. After years of feminism, hospitals and homes are still full of women who make attempts against their own lives or their mental stability, because they've been abandoned by their man or are incapable of abandoning their man. Nobody thinks of waving red flags round these silent deaths. Why? Because we can't attribute any ideal meaning to them? Because we can't abstract from the complex and confused personal reasons which caused these deaths?

Or we can turn the question round and ask: when is it that the death of an individual becomes a symbol or ethic (an ambiguous ethic, which praises life only in order to give new impulse to violence). I don't believe it's only a matter of place – the streets rather than the hospital and the home.

In the letters and articles in *LC* about the death of Walter Rossi it seemed to me I found the answer.

The creation of a symbol requires the use of very few, very simple and easily recognisable elements. The fewer the personal parts in the story, the greater the number of people who can identify with it (the real life of the individual – obscure, complex and inextricable in its apparent unity – discourages identification and accentuates distance and separation).

Walter is commemorated by the comrades with the images of eternal Sentiment, an age-old literature which has been so little analysed that it appears spontaneous and natural. Walter is 'a bleeding body', 'a cold, still corpse', a 'boy of 20, such a will to fight, so much anger and so much love of life', 'he wanted to laugh, talk, love, he wanted a better life.' Life-Death Anger and 'initiation into violent struggle', 'like a game, like a film'. The analyses of fascism and anti-fascism circulating in the movement today – what have they to do with these elementary, highly calculated myths and well-consolidated structures of the Historical Imaginary, which in reality inspire the political behaviour of thousands of people?

What is the use of clinging to an old, petty-bureaucratic political practice like the 'condemnation' or 'dissociation' from 'gratuitous violence', from the 'armed party'? Is it thinkable that a gesture so discredited by the use that the guardian-of-order political parties have always made of it, will today undo the fascination of the ancient myth or ethic linking Life and Death, Indignation and Violence?

Until we have the courage to give some political attention (both theoretical and practical) to Sentiment and the Imaginary, every condemnation of violence can only sound like a deliberate recall to conventionality, or like expediency.

However, as you said in the introduction to the 'Little Anthology', we're not starting from scratch: the political critique of sexuality, of the unconscious, has a history by now and is present in the movement. Those who are blind and deaf are probably so used to talking loudly from above that they don't notice that down in the stalls there are already a lot of people laughing.

Lea Melandri

Solitude is an ill with no respect

Milan

As usual, I read the paper today. About Cristiana's letter 'how difficult things are between the comrades' and the debate 'assistance and/or humanity' – I think the two things are closely tied up. Solitude is a determinant way of being.

It conditions a person's life and, too often, his or her choices: passivity towards the system, or an individual rebellion (because it's not always possible to express it collectively) which may lead to alienation (drugs, madness) or to mistaken choices in sex, politics or life.

We claim to be communists. We talk so much about communism, but we're incapable of practising it 'socially'. Comrades to what level of commitment? If you're one of those 'lucky ones' who are politically active 24 hours a day . . . you're 100 per cent . . . No. I can't quantify it and I don't want to.

I only understand that these 'lucky ones', besides forgetting the 'social', also and above all deny themselves. Our practice is purely 'political' – at demonstrations, in strikes, in interventions at work (if you make any) or in your organisation (if you're in one). But already in meetings and assemblies our social/political practice is faulty. The comrade who intervenes clumsily, describing his own – not very political – experiences, is received with intolerance.

Once the 'political' interlude is over we all go home to our problems and our solitude.

Of course our way of life today desocialises us, dehumanises us: always in a hurry, with no real social structure, always tensed against capital. But there's also a lack of courage in facing this problem, a fear of appearing 'christian', so I don't want to listen to your problems and I'm ashamed to talk about mine. We only accept feelings if they're 'communist' – we don't have friends, we have comrades. We accept feelings if they can be 'socialised': despair at a comrade's death, hatred for the class enemy. All other relationships are aseptic.

Then there's the group; a box made all in one piece, you can't take it in parts. Usually it's difficult, even painful, to get in, so often you don't even try. Living like this you can reach the point of not knowing whether the comrade you share (part of) your life with still represents love, or has become a drug to ward off loneliness. You feel you're misusing him but you need some way of venting your feelings, expressing your doubts, your new and confused ideas. He accepts you with all your contradictions. You don't have to fear a severe political, dialectical and aseptic judge who listens to you with indifference or irony.

We reject the family. But we don't know how to be alone. In fact it isn't natural. We're not worried about having fathers, mothers, husbands, daughters, relations. But solitude is inhuman.

Solitude is an ill which has no respect. It hits us all hard. It imprisons you. To be different isn't difficult. But to be alone is, especially in the movement.

Maria

Choosing what to do

Don't let's fool ourselves, there's no time for illusions, now we must choose to move forward. I don't want to say what we should choose, when, how or with whom, I just want to tell you about myself. Today I choose not to have a world centre to defend, to move towards or to conquer.

134

I don't need a meeting to wait for or a chairmanship to win.

I don't need a party as the centre of my ideas, nor a mountain to climb.

Today I've chosen a desire: not to live each day as though it were my last, not to die without having thought about what I would do tomorrow. Nobody can force me to throw my life away for a one-day belief, for an anger unrelated to my desire to live and my awareness that they are trying to deny me my life.

I choose not to need exorcisms that conceal my past, my militancy, my having been a political party – expropriated or expropriator of the capacity to live and build. I want to start from my needs, to understand reality through what I do. I want to learn a trade in which I no longer talk *for* others, but *about* others.

I've chosen to practise this trade on a daily newspaper not so unlike the others, a paper which has had bosses and is surrounded by aspiring bosses.

I've chosen to work for a paper which gives me the chance to discover a lot of people who don't need to wait for 'the party' to become an opposition. Young people, workers, women – the usual people who don't come to meetings, who don't need to come to these meetings, who you meet regularly only if you leave the lecture halls and come out into the world. Because the world goes on outside this university . . .

Today I choose to manage my own anger and the hatred I feel against those who kill my comrades, to decide for myself on which terrain to seek justice, to decide for myself who is responsible, accomplice or abstentionist. If I must exercise violence I want to exercise it with people who have respect for life, with people who don't have suicidal ideals to follow, with those who want to join their anger with mine for greater strength. I choose not to have ideals which oblige me to defend those who are no longer with me because they've decided to take over the struggle which is also mine, those who have declared private war, outside of history, both on states and on window panes, as though everything was something they have to fight against.

None of these things I've chosen gives me the certainty of victory nor of the road to follow, but I don't want to stand still waiting for someone or something which will put me on this road. Today every comrade can choose, together with others or alone,

135

to deal with his own life, even if this doesn't solve the problem of the ones who want to go on deciding, for everyone or in the name of everyone, the terrain, the objectives and the form of a battle in which they are already determined to be the generals.

There's one more thing we can decide today and I want to do it; it's not necessary to decide it for all time. That is, there's no need to have to do today what we did only yesterday.

Mauro

On 15 December 1976 the police entered a flat in the working-class district of Sesto San Giovanni (Milan). Walter Alasia, a 20-year-old ex-Lotta Continua activist, opened fire, killing two policemen and then tried to escape by jumping out of the window. He was shot dead by other policemen while lying on the ground.

Why don't we call them comrades?

Rome

I've wanted to write for a long time, ever since comrade Walter Alasia was executed in Milan by the 'forces of law and order'.

I didn't like the fact that an article affectionately commemorating a murdered comrade had to be signed (in this case by Guido Viale). I thought: funny that the editorial board doesn't agree with what Viale says. But then I thought: LC is in chaos now (it was after Rimini), so there'll be chaos at the newspaper too. So I didn't write.

Now they've killed three comrades in Germany (it's 'not clear' whether the four at Mogadishu were comrades or not, perhaps because they have no history) and not one of the many articles published in the paper has had the courage to call them 'comrades'.

It's as though some supervisor had systematically replaced this word with 'RAF militants', 'terrorists' in inverted commas, or their names and surnames.

You didn't even bring out the old line, 'we don't agree with their methods but they are still comrades.'

To me this seems really bad, very bad – I'll try to explain
136

why. First, when mistaken positions and practices emerge on the left, or ones which are difficult to justify in the face of public opinion, it's just taking the easy way out to consider them as not really belonging to the left itself. If we do this we risk forgetting that these divergent positions are a response to our own contradictions, different expressions of our own desire for communism. Particularly when we consider these positions to be mistaken, we must recognise their class-struggle origin in order to criticise them and go beyond them.

Secondly, I have the suspicion that this super-respectable distancing from the RAF serves to keep up the hard-won image of 'good sense' gained at Bologna. Although this may be understandable, given the present climate of repression, it remains absolutely unjustifiable; a good image in the bourgeois press doesn't help us in the struggle against repression. It's our capacity to organise and struggle, and so on and so forth, which will make us strong.

Carla

See note on page 24.

The ghost of non-communication

Bologna

This letter is for all the comrades at present doing military service who, like me, are unhappy both in the barracks and in their relations with the city folk and comrades. I read the letter from Salvatore published in *LC* (28 October) and I absolutely agree with what he says about still feeling an outsider after three years of 'serious' political militancy, not being accepted by those same comrades who make such good speeches about communism, equality and so on. I'm particularly interested in that 'ghost' which is 'stalking through the movement amongst the comrades', i.e. non-communication.

I want to tell you about my experiences in the barracks and in the town, here in Bologna, as a soldier and proletarian, an experience/violence which by now has become chronic and which

137

all conscripts feel. This violence has two faces. One is the violence you have to endure in the barracks, and I think that's the best known and most discussed. The other – more subtle – is the violence you experience in town when you're off duty (even if you're wearing civilian clothes) because you're unemployed and a southerner like me.

In town it's terrible. We often, in fact always, go out in a group and wander round piazza Maggiore where we are offended by the rich display in the shop windows. We feel like stray dogs during those few hours, often without a lira in our pockets. You experience a terrible paranoic isolation from absolutely everybody. And the worst is with the comrades, particularly the women who can't stand us because we represent that rottenest race of Italian males, i.e. soldiers.

So either you stay in the barracks and become even more alienated, or you reach the point of prostituting yourself, which I've done and everybody in my situation does. It isn't hard to find homosexuals outside the barracks and besides (that's the main point) they pay you as well. At least you get that, so you can even afford not to eat the filthy mess food occasionally.

And all of us – proletarians and outsiders, conscripted workers and unemployed, forced to this beggary and prostitution – besides having to put up with the daily heavy sexual repression and non-communication coming from the 'serious' comrades of Bologna, also live these horrible 12 months in a state of continual anxiety and worry about what we'll do afterwards, with all the problems of jobs which bloody well don't exist, with the fact that your family can't send you more money than they do, that transport costs and even the price of the bus ticket is a problem, that reorganisation has been put through in the barracks, and finally that the only real peace (the one positive note) is with the other comrades in the barracks, in the space we've created to struggle against the injustices and authoritarian shit that so many proletarians endure every year in the Italian lager-barracks. Let's keep this space open, 'serious' comrades. Long live communism.

A soldier comrade from the Viali barracks

One Monday at the end of October

Dear comrades,
Monday morning, waking up in the cold and fog. Getting up at six in the morning is a real violence, a little daily Stammheim running through your life in the prison of work.

It's that unsatisfied desire to sleep, to snuggle down and think unhurriedly about your life, your loves, your miseries in the warmth of your bed, 'splendid stage of dreams and love'.

Solitude of a dark dawn, suffocated by smoke, criss-crossed by chilly heavily-wrapped figures clinging to bicycle handlebars, scooters, steering wheels.

Smog-dirtied mist, suburban smells and colours, then at the city centre you change coaches (this morning I've managed to get a seat again).

The cold envelops and penetrates, swallowing up the last traces of warmth spread over your skin: not yet 7 o'clock and I'm already into the work-cycle.

I refuse to begin my days like this, nothing to do with me, the requirements of the office, the times of the alarm clock, I hate that bell! What do they want from me? A coach bringing me nearer and nearer to the office and all its accessories: worse than watching Sunday afternoon TV.

That's what refusal to work means: it isn't an idea, a myth, but this concrete need to stay in bed, strangle the alarm clock and take back time for yourself.

It's the need to rest body and mind. Images and sensations from a short journey to work, scribbled notes for a letter to the paper, looking for privacy.

The coach stops, I get out into the square, follow the portico, cross the road, the other portico. I'm there, open the window, begin. And I can't even go to the newsagent – it's Monday and the dear 'red paper' doesn't come out, I won't find it there amongst all the others.

Ciao,

A comrade

Oxygen

Ciao,

I'm a girl almost twenty-three years old who hasn't the right to consider herself, but nevertheless hopes soon to be called – at last – a comrade.

I need to be accepted, I have a terrible desire to really talk to other comrades, I need it and without exaggerating and/or appearing grotesque, I can say I absolutely must find it, like oxygen.

If you only knew the times I've walked past the Lotta Continua office in Bologna without having the courage to go in! It will probably seem silly, but I wouldn't know what to say and that's always been my great fear, being judged an outsider, an intruder, yes me! Me, with my bourgeois appearance sticking to me like a second skin and daily becoming more unbearable and uncomfortable; so I appear disgustingly integrated into the system and have to suffocate and deny my ideals when inside I feel a great longing to shout and rebel, and instead I find I'm such a coward! But I'll try and ask for help, I'll try today! Today I'm asking for help in taking off this mask I've been wearing for too long, help to stop despising myself for my own weakness and cowardice, help in breaking down all those pretences I've been hiding behind and which have brought me to this. Help, because I'm destroying myself, because I'm hurting myself too much, and now it's not even enough for me to cry help, even abnegation is hardly enough, because I don't exist and I hate myself. What am I? I haven't even the right to define myself a woman, I'm nothing, a nought, a zero. Help me, comrade, I need you and you will help, won't you? And not out of pity – perhaps you understand – but help me fit in, help me be myself, help me become a comrade!

I want to be a comrade!!! That's the only reason I'm still alive, because at the bottom of my soul, whole and unlimited, this desire lives. I still believe that madness is not the only way to find freedom!

S.O.S.

Movement

Florence

Dear comrades,

I remember when *Il Manifesto,* during the Rimini congress, wrote that Lotta Continua had become an 'American style movement' – in my opinion, without meaning to, they were paying you an enormous compliment. Even though I do understand that to be compared with Americans isn't usually pleasant. I'm an American comrade who's been active in LC since 1971. It was a hard struggle to get myself accepted by the comrades, firstly because I'm from the USA (understandable), secondly because I'm a woman (less understandable) and thirdly because I'm not beautiful (incomprehensible; the equivalent of not having a white skin).

Well, I overcame these barriers because I got the chance to have several open rows with all the comrades – something which wasn't possible in the '60s when I was active around the PSIUP (I say 'around' because the only women accepted by the PSIUP in those days were the wives and girlfriends of comrades, or women who did political work with a male mentality). The fact that LC is dealing, at its own expense, with its inner contradictions – the struggles of women, young people, gays – isn't pure chance. The majority of our comrades have understood that to go halfway with a revolution is very dangerous, that to give power to politically valid comrades who are also full of contradictions and bourgeois values can only be disastrous, because it would mean giving birth to a distorted socialism: the sort of socialism that would be produced by the PCI, which collaborates in evicting squatters to protect and defend private property. I'm convinced that until we become aware of the contradictions and bourgeois conditioning that affect each one of us, no socialism in an industrialised country can survive.

We mustn't forget that 'personal relationships' have always been practised in America, just as in Italy there's been the practice of politics. But now I have the feeling that something's changing. For example, I spent three months in New York this year and I was fortunate enough to meet the comrades from Columbia University who last year, by organised action and occupying the faculty, managed to keep Kissinger from taking a Chair the university

141

authorities had offered him. At the same time, in the state of Ohio about 200 students from Kent University occupied for a month the ground where four students were shot dead in 1970 by the US National Guard, during a protest against the Vietnam bombings. They occupied that ground today because the university authorities want to build a gym there, cancelling once and for all the memory of the fallen comrades. But the great thing, in my opinion, is that in 1970 these 200 students were only eleven years old – that would be normal in Italy, but this happened in the USA. And don't let's forget the 'black out' in New York last August, the mass expropriation of goods by blacks and Puerto Ricans. That's not enough, I know, and the road to political consciousness for Americans is still very long, just as the road to personal consciousness will be very long for Italians. The important thing for me is that there are American comrades who have understood that it isn't enough to practise only the 'personal', that it's *also* necessary to organise politically. And it's great to know that the Italian comrades of Lotta Continua have understood that it isn't enough to practise politics, that it's *also* necessary to practise the 'personal' . . .

Gloria Ramakus

Land

Montisi (Sienna)

We are anarchist comrades from Turin and we'd like to explain our situation as briefly as possible.

We've come to Tuscany in order to live in the country, farm the land, be a bit happier in fact than in that absurd paranoia called the city. Now we're in the shit, we've already been fucked over once: thrown out of a farm we'd taken as share-croppers. Now we've landed up somewhere else, another con, no contract, no security, no anything. The 'owner' wants to evict us and soon we'll be out in the road. We don't want to go back to Turin, stand in those endless queues at the labour-exchange, stamp the pink form, desperately look for a house (we have a one-year-old baby). All this is really bad.

We believe in the *land* and we want, or rather we're trying, to find a place with some land where we can finally live in peace.

142

Now we're asking you (any part of Italy, it's all the same to us): if you know of any farms for rent, please let us know. We know that they are very hard to find, because of the shit laws in this country. Anyway, we are prepared to join comrades squatting on uncultivated land, so please write to us.

You're squatting on this land, but we don't know exactly where to find you, so anybody who has anything to tell us, please do, and anyone who wants to come and see us, please do, especially comrades from Sienna.

NB. We're pretty desperate! Communist greetings,

Oliviero, Paola and the little male Saverio

A lonely Witch

Rome

Dear comrades,
I'm writing because I feel bloody lonely. Before I went in for politics I thought a comrade couldn't feel alone, that she never had time, that she was always together with people she could communicate with, that she didn't know what solitude meant.

Then I discovered that all this is absolutely untrue, I discovered (obviously through personal experience) that even a comrade can feel alone, yes, even the comrade who is always ready to struggle has moments when she's not thinking that the police are out there shooting, that there are so many comrades in jail, she's not thinking that at 5 p.m. there's the assembly in the Women's House, and she couldn't care less that the cabinet is deciding on more repressive measures; there are moments when even the 'activist' comrade thinks only about whether it's more tragic to commit suicide by throwing oneself from the third floor, swallowing tranquillizers or turning on the gas (and then unfortunately you think that a guaranteed way of dying is to go and distribute leaflets in front of a fascist HQ). But then you remember that in fact your suicide would be a murder because there's someone who wants to destroy you, who wants to eliminate you because you've acquired consciousness and are struggling for something right. Then you decide that killing yourself is bloody stupid and so you start again, struggling, going to the assembly at

143

the Women's House and the meetings of the neighbourhood committee.

Greetings with a clenched fist from a lonely Witch!

Ciccia

In practice . . . I'm expecting you

Bologna

Ciao,

I'm a Lotta Continua sympathiser. For some time I've been reading in the paper appeals from comrades who feel lonely and desperate. For god's sake, people, what are we doing? Is it such an effort to give them a hand, help someone who's struggling in the shit, etc . . .?

OK, I don't say that we should take over other people's problems (for one thing we're not all made the same way), but trying to solve or at least help the problem of loneliness is as important – if not more important – than political work. Otherwise what are we supposed to be doing? Not practising what we preach?

I live in the country 14 kilometres from Bologna. Anyone who wants to come and see me, write (I haven't got a telephone but I've got a lot of friends). That goes for the 'lonely Witch' as well.

Greetings with a clenched fist,

Ruggero

PS. Giving people a bed for a few nights is no problem. Ruggero Gianicola – via Frate Giovanni 33 – Ozzano Emilia (Bologna)

Evelyn Home?

Comrades,

What is this? a new form of consciousness raising? The moaning mass letter as a new form of alternative practice? Couldn't it just be that these 'new' subjects have been aired so often in small and big groups, and have become so rhetorical, that those same groups are fed up to the teeth with hearing about them,

144

so in order to go on feeling satisfied with oneself and with the progress of 'revolutionary humanism', there's the 'need' (never forget to sanctify 'needs'!) to write to the paper? Marvellous exercises, we're capable of sounding the whole range of human feelings! But if we're so good at breaking through the barriers of the 'personal', why does all the solitude remain, why are our lives still made difficult or impossible by frigidity or impotence, by the extreme, unpleasant and unmentionable problems (the confessional letters never go as far as to mention them) which afflict 'revolutionaries' as well? Sure, because if we do some introspection instead of consciousness raising, we discover that despite all the good will and hard work we're never 'free' or fully realised, down at the bottom there's probably a bit of fascism left, ready to re-emerge in the future, after we've taken over power, and destroy our imaginary 'beautiful' revolution.

Comrades, we've had enough of ideology, enough of *false* consciousness, personal problems are overcome or not (maybe one just feels a little better) with individual or group experiences. (Aren't we comrades? Then we should try to talk with everybody, not just amongst ourselves.) But they are overcome not only by talking about them or thanks to the holy grace of 'true communism'. Do we seriously believe that these alternative confessional practices bring communism closer than a successful strike or demonstration, than getting a comrade out of jail with our struggle, than a growing consciousness amongst the masses of the need to bring down the bourgeois state and take political power (that's a bit less than making a revolution, it isn't enough to bring it about, but it's a necessary condition, as history teaches us; and in the past, to reach this 'minimum objective' everybody got together, even if they weren't 'perfect', 'liberated' comrades).

Some of us still have parts in their personal lives which are 'secret' rather than 'political' (well, sometimes not all the good will, the class choice and the communist hugs and kisses are enough to overcome the neuroses!) but is someone who participates in the struggle a communist or not? Will someone who every now and then doesn't 'think in a revolutionary way', and so falls into the sin of lese-communism, be excluded from the 'communist paradise' unless he repents? Are there 'sins of thought' for communists as well? Is communism only for the pure of heart?

145

A very 'impure', and perhaps heretical communist –
an aetheist, really (is he a non-comrade? and what is a
comrade?) from Messina

PS. Isn't a page of moans too much for the finances of the paper? Or does it increase circulation, like the Evelyn Home pages in the bourgeois magazines?

Sexuality in the bus

Naples

Dear comrades,
I want to set out a particular problem I have. Practically from the beginning, my prevalent form of expressing my sexuality has been leaning against girls on crowded buses.

This is part of the violence that women are daily submitted to, but also of the violence of a life (mine) without love and full of humiliations (coming from women, too).

I leave it to the comrades. I think it might be useful for me to discuss this problem personally with a feminist group.

Marcello

Whose comrade?

Bologna, 2.30 a.m.

But how many comrades have really understood what this business of personal and political is all about?

I'd often thought of writing to you but I never had the courage, just like Cristiana (*LC*, 14 October). In fact, it's to the discussion started by her letter that I want to contribute. To say that I'm alone and desperate too. To say that like S.O.S., who lives in the same town as me, I've often thought of going to Lotta Continua headquarters and saying: 'Hi, I'm a bloke who agrees with you and I'd like to carry on the struggle for communism together with you', but I've never had the courage to do it either (my fear may appear perfectly absurd to you, but that's just the point: how many comrades have understood the – true – 'story' of the personal-being-political?)

146

Yes, fear: on the one hand, of not being accepted or being looked at with heavy suspicion (and immediately afterwards having necessarily to climb up to the top of the first eight-storey building to end it all); on the other, of being put to the 'quality' test at the first meeting on the general political situation and being asked to make an 'organic contribution', me who am only a dummy who can't make a long political speech, who never spoke at the school assemblies (I finished school two years ago with my nice little certificate and now I'm only an ultra-excluded unemployed person).

I'm writing to ask those 'komrades' (the new 'new' police) who talk about 'lonely hearts columns' or 'Evelyn Home': but what was it that brought you to sympathise with the ideas and objectives of the revolutionary movement and become 'political activists' in the first place?

Wasn't it because of a 'personal' sense of discomfort? In my case, everything started when – about four years ago – I started to feel really uncomfortable in the sort of life I had to live. I began questioning the hypocrisy of so-called 'normal' behaviour based on false individualistic 'values', and trying to relate to other people who were less squalid and alienating, in fact communists. So I acquired a (political) consciousness that in order to overthrow this model of life on a social scale it was – and is – necessary to struggle against capital whose institutions impose this oppressive everyday existence on us, to make us submit to the logic of profit and exploitation. I realised that my 'personal' discomfort was an enormously 'political' fact.

I began to spend time with some comrades and go to their meetings: but I couldn't identify with that way of 'doing politics' the way one 'does' work: I found they were largely living out the same bourgeois roles and conventions that I was trying to shake off. The only 'human' relationship I had with them was that now and then they asked me to make a 'general speech', which I was no good at and so got excluded. But how can you talk about 'general' things when what you really want is to get to know the people who are around you, touch them, talk to them about your common problems, your miseries, your relationship with the parents you have to live with and who obstinately try to make you accept their model 'family-work-home-what will people say'. But no: only a

147

bureaucratic way of relating (and these are comrades in the revolutionary left); but christ, comrades, we're struggling for communism in society, why don't we try and practise it amongst ourselves in the meantime? I left after a few months without anyone noticing. Then military service, which paradoxically was almost a relief in this mess: and here I am again, an LC 'sympathiser' with a great desire to meet other comrades because it's absurd that I should call myself a comrade at the moment (whose comrade am I?) so here I am, more desperate than ever and with an awful sense of futility. You understand me, don't you comrades (or rather, Evelyn Homes)? Please give me a hand, give me the hope that my being a revolutionary isn't going to be for ever limited to buying *LC* every day and voting for the furthest-left candidates at the elections every few years; help me to understand how much 'political' there is in my personal.

With tear-filled eyes (yes, even males cry). I need oxygen, too.

Lots of love to everybody,

Gianni

New Year 1978

Naples

Dear Mum and Dad,
We children want to be good and stop worrying you during the coming year, so we promise we'll behave the way you'd like us to.

Your 18-year-old eldest child, when she hops into bed with the thirtieth person, will take care not to get pregnant for the third time; she'll stop riding around with four people on her scooter, she'll try to go to school at least once a week and she won't smoke joints on top of tranquillizers so as not to vomit again and make Mum clean up the mess which is such hard work for her.

Your 16-year-old second child will try to improve his imitations of Dad when he blows his top and stammers with rage, he'll try to collect all the idiotic things Mum says neatly in an album instead of telling his friends whenever it comes up; he won't
148

masturbate the cat with pencils but promises to personally satisfy the sexual needs of all the household pets; instead of digging holes in the wall with his fingers in moments of desperation, he'll use the drill; he'll stop burning Mum's mail-order catalogues before she has a chance to intercept them.

Finally, your youngest child promises that he won't get caught stealing trousers in chain-stores any more, and he'll avoid the ones where they've already got him listed so as not to end up in a reformatory, following the kind promises of all the supermarket managers where he's been nicked; he won't swear in Sicilian in front of his 80-year-old great-aunt, but will translate his obscenities into perfect Italian in order to give the dear old lady a useful lesson. He'll stop smoking his friends' cigarettes and will personally buy his own Gauloises; instead of shouting 'Autonomia operaia' at demonstrations he'll get down to making explosive devices to be placed in embassies and fascist HQs; he'll stop telling his friends that you're utter fools and will help his brother and sister in compiling the album recording your most idiotic moments; finally, since smoking Lebanese red [hash] gives him unfortunate attacks of diarrhoea, he promises to go on to heroin or acid, whichever you prefer, so that he won't be a nuisance any more with his nocturnal complaints of stomach ache.

These are only a few of the good deeds your children promise to do to make you happy in the coming year. It's so wonderful to spend a joyful New Year in the Christian peace and warmth of the family circle, where perfect harmony reigns between us children and you parents – we have no secrets from you, thanks to the serene family atmosphere in this house and the excellent way you've brought us up, and never shocking us with immoral talk about sex, concentrating instead on the stork and the family cult. Since we were small you taught us that we mustn't speak to just anybody, like those bad children out in the street do, so we happily spent our whole infancy in the safety of your house illuminated by your comforting presence. The sound education received has inculcated in us most particularly a sense of modesty, and now you are reaping the harvest of what you've done to make good citizens of us. So once more we sincerely wish you a happy New Year, and promise you that if this loving letter gives you a heart attack, we'll break open our piggy-banks and willingly spend all our pennies on

149

paying to get you into an old people's home or a psychiatric hospital.

Lots of love from your cherubs,

1) Aqi 59
2) Alloween 61
3) Giufà 63

1) Pseudonym of daughter no. 1, author of this letter, activist in the revolutionary left, (18).
2) Pseudonym of son no. 2, ex-activist, now looking around, (16).
3) Pseudonym of son no. 3, anarchoid, (14).

PS. Dear comrades, this letter was written in a moment of abjection and vileness produced by the boredom and rage accumulated during the Christmas holidays in a perfectly ordinary bourgeois family. I hope you'll publish it as an example of the enormous gap existing between parents and children, between what they'd like us to do and what we really experience without their knowledge. It would be amusing if everybody gave 'Mum and Dad' a little letter containing the truth about our everyday life, so very different from their ideas; but on the other hand, I don't think a collective heart attack of parents would solve the extremely difficult problem of the family as vehicle for ideology-repression-roles-neuroses for all. That's why I'm not putting this letter under Dad's plate, but sending it to you instead. I apologize for not using the traditional glitter christmas paper with hosts of fluttering cherubs.

Ciao.